THE MYSTERY OF CULTURE CONTACTS, HISTORICAL RECONSTRUCTION, AND TEXT ANALYSIS: AN EMIC APPROACH

THE MYSTERY OF CULTURE CONTACTS, HISTORICAL RECONSTRUCTION, AND TEXT ANALYSIS: AN EMIC APPROACH

by

KENNETH L. PIKE,
GARY F. SIMONS, CAROL V. MCKINNEY, DONALD A. BURQUEST

Edited and introduced

by

KURT R. JANKOWSKY
Georgetown University

GEORGETOWN UNIVERSITY PRESS
WASHINGTON, DC

Georgetown University Press, Washington, D.C.
© 1996 by Georgetown University Press. All rights reserved.
Printed in the United States of America

10 9 8 8 7 6 5 4 3 2 1   1996

Library of Congress Cataloging-in-Publication Data

Pike, Kenneth Lee, 1912-
    The mystery of culture contacts, historical reconstruction and
    text analysis : an emic approach / Kenneth L. Pike [in association
    with] Carol V. McKinney, Gary F. Simons, and Donald A. Burquest ;
    Kurt R. Jankowsky, editor.
        p.   cm.
    Includes bibliographical references.
    Contents: Toward the historical reconstruction of matrix patterns
    in morphology / Kenneth L. Pike and Gary F. Simmons -- Understanding
    misunderstanding as cross-cultural emic clash / Kenneth L. Pike and
    Carol V. McKinney -- The importance of purposive behavior in text
    analysis / Kenneth L. Pike and Donald A. Burquest.
        1. Linguistics.   I. Jankowsky, Kurt R.   II. Title.
P125.P54   1995
410--dc20
ISBN 0-87840-295-0   95-14739

CONTENTS

EDITOR'S INTRODUCTION

1. Preliminary Remarks

2. On Kenneth L. Pike
2.1 *Publications and Nature of Research*
2.2 *University Studies and Professional Careers*
2.3 *Recognition and Honors Received*
2.4 *Nomination for the Nobel Peace Prize*
2.5 *Tagmeme and the -etic/-emic Principle*
2.6 *Teamwork among SIL Researchers*

3. On Donald A. Burquest

4. On Carol V. McKinney

5. On Gary F. Simons

6. On this Publication

1. *Preliminary Remarks*

Every book has its history. Telling of how a book originated is frequently restricted to casual oral communication, for instance, among a few coworkers who were instrumental in converting a casual idea into a practical and workable procedure. To talk about the why and the how in a more formal way seems almost unavoidable if an author like Kenneth L. Pike is involved.

Georgetown University, most specifically its School of Languages and Linguistics, has been very fortunate to have had Dr. Pike as a frequent visitor to—and as an invariably active participant in—numerous functions which dealt, naturally, with linguistic subject matter. On one of such occasions a few years ago I raised with him the question as to whether he would agree to have a monograph published consisting exclusively of papers written by him. I felt that such a book would be of considerable interest not only for the linguistic experts, but also for the much larger group of people whose intellectual curiosity would include the desire to get a glimpse of what sophisticated methods of language study could and should achieve. I was convinced that Georgetown University Press would be very much interested in publishing such a volume.

The response to my question was favorable as far as Dr. Pike was concerned, and Georgetown University Press likewise agreed to my suggestion. After that it did not take very long for a solid plan to evolve. One of the two papers of the proposed volume would be the English version an article that had already appeared in a Russian translation (cf. Pike and Simons 1993). The second paper would be written in accordance with a special topical request outlined by me (cf. the second paper in this volume). There was from early on also agreement with Dr. Pike as to a third paper, but its subject matter was to be determined at a later stage.

Things developed smoothly in the months to follow. Georgetown University Press gave me a firm commitment for a speedy publication, and Dr. Pike and his co-authors supplied the manuscripts well within the anticipated time frame. To prepare the camera-ready copy was not as easy and could not be done as speedily as one would want optimistically to hope, but the delay remained within reasonable limits.

Special thanks are due to the authors for their great cooperation and to Georgetown University Press, especially to its Director, Dr. John Samples.

2. *On Kenneth L. Pike*

2.1 *Publications and Nature of Research*

The publications of Kenneth L. Pike are uniquely impressive in numerous respects. Their quantity, which certainly would be large enough for a dozen of scholars to bypass the hurdle of tenure and promotion without a hitch, is by no means the most significant factor. There are several others that deserve mentioning for much more important reasons. They are intrinsically related to the uniqueness of his personality and the many special conditions under which his professional career took shape. Only some of them can be referred to here, but they are likely to be a sufficient illustration for the unusual and highly remarkable elements that characterize almost every stage of his professional and personal life.

First and foremost, Pike's linguistic research is tied to a very practical pursuit. As a matter of fact, the practical aspect was and is the indispensable basis for his theoretical interests. He launched his professional career in the mid-1930s under extraordinary circumstances: striving to become a translator which involved a language that he was about to learn, and to learn it at that in the most effective—if not also the hardest—way by living for many years among the native inhabitants. In 1934 W. Cameron Townsend, who "had translated the New Testament for the Cakchiquel-speaking people of Guatemala" (cf. Eunice Pike 1981:14), and Leonard L. Legters, who had done missionary work among the Comanche Indians (ibid.), had founded 'Camp Wycliffe' for the purpose of training young students to translate the Bible into languages mostly known only to their native speakers. The prospectus for the course informed the applicants "that the student would be taught, among other things, the description of an Indian language, some anthropology, and a short course in phonetics" (Eunice Pike 1981:13). The Camp started out with two students. When Pike joined a year later in 1935, there were still only five. Today 'Camp Wycliffe' has grown into the 'Summer Institute of Linguistics' (SIL), headquartered in Arlington, TX, with some 2,250 staff members, most of them doing research, some of them serving in other capacities, such as training, consulting, and doing administrative work. According to Dr. Frank Robbins, the current President of SIL:

> Another 300 plus are currently in preparation toward serving as field linguists, either in training or developing their support base. SIL field linguists have been directly involved with research on nearly 1500 languages in more than 50 countries. Currently they are working with approximately 1000 language projects. (Robbins 1995:58)

Quite apart from the significance that the SIL has gained as a missionary institution, the importance of its work for the advancement of linguistic research in general is beyond all comparison. The projects

> are noteworthy because of the types of languages involved: many of them are spoken by fewer than 10,000 people, do not exist in written form, and have never been studied by outsiders. The missionaries who take on the enormous

task of producing Scripture in these languages become crack linguists. They
are the largest army of field linguists in the world, equipped with state-of-the-
art linguistic software running on battery or solar-powered laptop computers.
And although the translators themselves earn only a pittance, funding for these
projects tops $100 million a year. (Weiss 1995:37)

It seems that Pike has always been far too active as to be content with
devoting his time to only one professional pursuit. After the brief training
session at 'Camp Wycliffe' during the Summer of 1935, he went to Mexico
and started his life among the Mixtec Indians at San Miguel, a small village
in Mixtec country. He learned their language, got totally immersed in their
culture, gained the respect and friendship of most of those with whom he
came into contact, and served for all of them as a reliable helper in count-
less cases of hardship and need. After all, he had followed a vocation rather
than carrying out the duties of an ordinary profession. During those seven
years of 'village life', Pike, his wife Evelyn and growing family had to
shoulder numerous burdens and to live up to many challenges. In spite of
frustrations and disappointments they fulfilled their mission and experienced
a great deal of satisfaction and enjoyment in the process.

The summers were spent in the United States, mostly by teaching at
'Camp Wycliffe'—which soon developed into the 'Summer Institute of
Linguistics' under its founder and first General Director W. Cameron
Townsend—but also by studying linguistics and, at the suggestion of
Cameron Townsend, attending courses at the Linguistic Institute of the Lin-
guistic Society of America [= LSA], which were conducted during the summer months. Thus Pike came into contact with a great number of the
foremost American linguists of the time such as Bernard Bloch, Leonard
Bloomfield, Charles Carpenter Fries, Zellig S. Harris, Edward Sapir, Edgar
H. Sturtevant, George Trager, and many others. Pike's expertise in phonetics, acquired both by his own practical work with the Mixtec Indians and
by intensively studying every bit of published material on the subject that
he could lay his hands on, did not fail to impress all those linguists who
had become aware of his newly obtained knowledge. George Trager, for
instance, reviewing Pike's book on phonetics (cf. Pike 1943)—his third
major publication on the subject—had this to say: "Phonetics is so young
a branch of science that it is still true that most phoneticians are self-taught.
Pike, however, has taught himself so well that from now on the rest of us
can go to him for the basic knowledge we need" (Trager 1943:16).

By his relationship to the Wycliffe Bible Translators and the Summer
Institute of Linguistics Pike was also keenly interested in the purely religious aspect of his work. This led inevitably to a large number of religious
writings, books as well as articles. The first books of this kind date back to
the mid-forties and are written in Mixteco or bilingually in Mixteco-Spanish

(cf. Brend 1987:11). As in the case of his linguistic publications, these writings are intrinsically related to his practical work and his particular style of life. A book such as the following, published in 1962, may illustrate this point: *With Heart and Mind: A Personal Synthesis of Scholarship and Devotion*. The interpenetration of professional and personal-religious life remained the central motive throughout Pike's career, and it continued even after his retirement, as is indicated in the most recent of his religious books, written together with Hugh Steven and published in 1989: *Pike's Perspectives: An Anthology of Thought, Insight, and Moral Purpose*.

As a man of letters, Pike could be expected to be interested in poetry. And this is indeed the case. That he is, however, also extremely fond of writing poetry himself, is certainly quite unusual for a linguistic scholar. One might, furthermore, be particularly surprised to realize that Pike attempts to align poetry with linguistics and also poetry with religion. Yet not to do so would be totally uncharacteristic for him. In everything Pike does, he embraces a holistic approach. For Pike there are no parts that can exist in isolation: they have to be viewed as parts of an overreaching structure of which the parts are the constitutive components. In accordance with this attitude his linguistic procedures always aim at language as a whole. While the separate investigation of individual sections of language is necessary and unavoidable, such a piecemeal research is but an intermediary stage and, in his opinion, has to be conducted within an overall theoretical framework in which each part is assigned its interrelational position. He elaborates on his thoughts in this regard in his influential work on *Language in Relation to a Unified Theory of the Structure of Human Behavior*, first published in 1955 in two parts comprising a total of 250 pages. Its second revised edition of 1967 was enlarged to 762 pages. His procedure is not basically different when he focuses on what common ground linguistics and poetry on the one hand and poetry and religion on the other do actually share. He wrote, for instance, papers in which he investigates certain elements in a poem which he had determined to be of importance linguistically (cf. "A Poem on Disconnecting Form and Meaning" ([1976]). His paper "Language – Where Science and Poetry Meet" (1965) is another example of his eagerness to stress the fundamental interrelationship of linguistics and literature. He even demonstrates how a linguist who writes poetry can subject his own poems to a thorough linguistic analysis (cf. "Towards the Linguistic Analysis of One's Own Poems" [1983]).

2.2 *University Studies and Professional Careers*

In Charles Carpenter Fries, of the University of Michigan, director of the 1937 Linguistic Institute of the LSA, Pike had found an ardent academic sponsor who urged him to work for his Ph. D. degree in linguistics. This recommendation was based on Fries's high opinion of what Pike had accomplished so far—apart from his practical achievements—in theoretical linguistic studies. Fries had invited Pike to give a luncheon presentation on "The Problem of Tones in Mexican Indian Languages" during the 1938 Summer Institute of the LSA. The 90-minute lecture was attended by a number of well-known linguists, including Edgar Sturtevant and Leonard Bloomfield. Eunice Pike reports on that decisive event:

> The paper was very well received and to this day Ken remembers with gratitude the encouragement the men gave him. Professor Sturtevant said, "There's a lot of work done there," and when Professor Bloomfield had occasion to write to Ken later, he said, "I learned a great deal from your account of Mixtec." (Eunice Pike 1981:82)

Fries went even one big step further and equated Pike's presentation with a doctoral thesis. Since Pike was not in a position to take part in regular coursework even during the summers, due to his obligations with the Mixtec Indian project and his teaching duties at the SIL, Fries negotiated special arrangements with the University of Michigan, so that Pike was permitted to take courses only during the summer and would get credit even for courses which he could attend only part of the time.

After completion of his thesis, entitled *A Reconstruction of Phonetic Theory* (Pike 1941), he presented himself for the oral examination in August of 1941.

With the Ph.D. being officially awarded to him in 1942, Pike was the first SIL staff member who had obtained this degree. From that time onward his professional life proceeded along two different lines. On the one hand, he had started an academic career at the University of Michigan, first on a part-time basis in various capacities from 1942 to 1947, then, until 1953, as Associate Professor of Linguistics, and subsequently as a Full Professor until 1977. He also served as Chairman of the Department of Linguistics from 1975 to 1977 and for one year simultaneously as Director of the English Language Institute, the prestigious institution founded in 1941 with Charles Carpenter Fries, Robert Lado, and Albert H. Marckwardt serving successively as its first directors.

On the other hand, Pike remained on the staff of the Summer Institute of Linguistics and of the Wycliffe Bible Translators. The roles he played there since he joined in 1935 are difficult to describe exhaustively. He continued to do field work in various parts of the world, trained at headquarters young field workers to prepare them linguistically for their arduous task, helped establish and maintain contact with governmental and professional institutions nationally and internationally—whose cooperation was vital for the maximally effective functioning of the Institute—and did administrative work on a large scale. For 37 years, from 1942 to 1979, he was President of the Summer Institute of Linguistics. The magnitude of the responsibilities which this position placed upon him, their significance for the SIL as well as for the larger linguistic community, and the dynamic vigor with which he went to work were widely recognized from early on. In 1947 the Linguistic Society of America passed a resolution in which it was stated

> that the members of the Linguistic Society present at the Summer Meeting having heard a report by Professor Kenneth Pike on the teaching in practical phonemics carried on at the Summer Institute of Linguistics at Norman, Oklahoma, and on the impressive series of publications appearing from the pens of its staff members, it is the sense of this group that the work of the group [...] should be strongly commended by our Society and welcomed as one of the most promising developments in applied linguistics in this country. (Cf. Eunice Pike 1981:138)

2.3 Recognition and Honors Received

It must be viewed as a special personal tribute to Professor Pike that the Linguistic Society of America elected him President for 1961. An equally great distinction is the fact that the Linguistic Association of Canada and the United States made him its President for 1977-78.

Of the large number of honors conferred on him nationally and internationally only a few can be mentioned here. When he was awarded the Charles Carpenter Fries Professorhip of Linguistics at the University of Michigan in 1974, the citation read by Dean Rhodes proclaimed that "Professor Pike's accomplishments and contributions to the field of linguistics coupled with his lifelong originality and energetic activity verge on the legendary" (cf. Eunice Pike 1981:176).

Many universities awarded him honorary degrees, for instance in America, Huntington College (Doctor of the Humanities, 1967), University of Chicago (Doctor of Humane Letters, 1973), and Georgetown University (Doctor of Humane Letters, 1984), and abroad, L'Université Réné Descartes (Sorbonne), Paris (Docteur Honoris Causa, 1978), and Albert-Ludwig Universität Freiburg, Germany (Doctor of Philosophy, 1993).

The title of President-Emeritus of the SIL, conferred on him at the time of his retirement in 1979, should not give rise to the mistaken belief that since then Dr. Pike has significantly curtailed his activities. There is ample evidence that to this very day he has no intention of calling it quits. He continued to travel throughout the country and around the globe, in order to participate in meetings, respond to invitations, or fulfill specific assignments by the SIL. His writing activity shows no letting up either. On the contrary, it seems to continue to spread out and intensify especially in the field of poetry. *Pike's Poems*, a volume of about 600 poems never before published, is about to be appear, most probably in 1995.

2.4 *Nomination for the Nobel Peace Prize*

In 1982 a special ceremony took place in Washington, DC. Its purpose was to celebrate the nomination of Dr. Pike for the Nobel Peace Prize. On that occasion Alan J. Dixon, US Senator (D-Illinois), stated the following:

> Dr. Pike's career, aided by the nearly 4,000 volunteers of the SIL, at the cost of oversimplification, boils down to this: Working in some 900 (nine hundred) previously unknown minority languages in more than 30 countries on five continents, this linguist and this institution have, by creating literacy via scientific phonology, alerted millions of human beings to their birthright of equality in world citizenship. [...]
>
> Dr. Pike [...] has become one of the world's foremost authorities on linguistics in general. [...] His methodology of creating a romanized script alphabet through phonetics for a previously unwritten language has set an international standard that will not be surpassed in this century or the next. (Makkai, 1983:10)

Equally strong language of support was used by Congressman Paul Simon as the Chairman of the US House Committee on Postsecondary Education:

> Dr. Kenneth L. Pike, President-Emeritus of the Summer Institute of Linguistics [...] has been the creative genius behind much of the enormous scientific production of SIL, as well as an inspirational leader of their dedication to the minority language groups of the world.
> (Makkai, 1983:13)
>
> I hereby officially nominate The Summer Institute of Linguistics and its President-Emeritus, Dr. Prof. Kenneth Lee Pike, as the Nobel Prize candidates for the year 1983. No other individual or group has done more for some of the most downtrodden of the world.
>
> The Summer Institute of Linguistics and Dr. Kenneth L. Pike are working for World Peace and Democracy directly through the communication-revolution that their literacy program generates. I urge you to award them the Nobel Peace Prize in 1983. (Ibid., 15)

These two quotations are excerpts from letters, dated January 5, 1983, addressed to the Norwegian Nobel Peace Prize Committee.

The outpouring of support from Dr. Pike's professional peers was no less forceful. The group of sponsors includes past presidents of the Linguistic Society of America (Charles F. Hockett, Cornell University), past presidents of the Linguistic Association of Canada and the Unites States (Sydney M. Lamb, Rice University), presidents of colleges (Gordon J. van

Wylen, Hope College) and universities (Frank H.T. Rhodes, Cornell University) as well as numerous distinguished scholars from other countries (André Martinet, Sorbonne; David C.C. Li, National Taiwan Normal University, and Ming Liu, The Chinese University of Hong Kong).

By 1993 he had been nominated for the Nobel Peace Prize for the 11th consecutive year (cf. Kaye 1994:291).

2.5 Tagmeme and the -etic/-emic Principle

In the course of his approximately six decades of professional life Pike has been the initiator of numerous practical procedures and theoretical approaches in the field of linguistics and language study. Thus, in a paper of 1964 entitled "Beyond the Sentence," he zoomed in on the 'notion beyond the sentence' at a time when hardly any linguist had realized that the days of the conventional 'sentence grammar' were certainly numbered and that a new dimension, as it were, was emerging and would develop before long into what was to be called 'text grammar', in relation to which the sentence grammar of yesteryears needed substantial redefinition.

Perhaps the most notable of the many innovations brought about by the pioneering efforts of Dr. Pike is the introduction of the -etic/-emic dichotomy into linguistics and the development of a methodology which provided the tools for its most effective application. The key terms had been around for a considerable time (cf. Morris Swadesh, "The Phonemic Principle," [1934]), but until then they had not yet been used in accordance with a systematically developed terminology. An -etic analysis focuses on the material aspect of language. It identifies and investigates all speech sounds occurring in any language. The -emic analysis, on the other hand, is exclusively concerned with the language-specific **functional** aspect of language units.

As the larger framework for the **functional** -emic investigation Pike created the *tagmemic theory*. He described its origin in these words: "Tagmemics of the Pikean type grew out of a 1949 question relating phonemics to grammar, following the learning of a language monolingually" (Pike 1995b:101). The experienced need to work monolingually led inevitably to some essential consequences:

- He had to study culture simultaneously with language.
- He had to combine the study of form and meaning, "not just formal structure, and not just abstract semantics" (ibid.).
- He had to take note, for very practical reasons, "which sounds made a difference in [...] meanings, and hence were linguistically contrastive" (ibid.).
- He had to embrace a holistic approach which involves "the interlocking [...] of all hierarchies, and all kinds of meanings and all

kinds of levels or domains – within human behavior as a whole, thus involving language, physical action, and philosophical abstractions and religious ones" (p. 102).

– He had to pay "attention to the need for GENERAL, UNIVERSAL components, within which there were VARIABLE LOCAL components. This led to the need for terms for the differences – for which I coined the words ETIC (from a GENERALIZED PHONETIC academic SYSTEM) and EMIC (coined from the PARTICULARIZED PHONEMIC UNITS)" (ibid.).

Tagmemics started out with phonology. It was soon expanded to include grammar. Next, reference was added. "FOUR COMPONENTS OF CLASS (SET), SLOT (POSITION), ROLE (FUNCTION), AND COHESION (AGREEMENT CONSTRAINTS) ARE RELEVANT TO EACH OF THE HIERARCHIES OF GRAMMAR, PHONOLOGY, AND REFERENCE" (103).

The development continued. This is illustrated best in the various editions of his *Language in Relation to a Unified Theory of the Structure of Human Behavior* (1955a, 1960, and 1967). Its seems to have reached its latest stage so far in a proclamation which Pike has made in a discussion on the occasion of the *Edward Sapir Centenary Conference* of 1984 in Ottawa:

Is there a cultural alphabet? Yes. Is there a general, innate underlying structure which is universal? An etic alphabet we can use? Yes. Is there a specific emics for each culture, one at a time following up that material to make it specific for each culture? Yes. Is there a locus of the culture, related to work of Sapir, and in relation to his kind of emic structure? Yes. (Pike in Cowan 1986:552)

2.6 *Teamwork among SIL Researchers*

We live in an age where overspecialization is almost as much of an unavoidable need as it is also a grave danger. Closest possible cooperation among researchers is one—and probably the most effective—strategy to overcome the drawbacks that inevitably accompany the career of the specializing expert.

In the Summer Institute of Linguistics teamwork seems to be practiced to a much wider extent than is usual in comparable institutions. It would, however, be too simplistic to attribute the strong desire of SIL research workers to tackle certain tasks as a team to the mere academic and scientific advantages that it would in all likelihood entail. What binds the group together are also shared academic and scientific objectives, but even more important than those are shared goals which transcend all scientific and academic pursuits. The linguistic effort is always motivated by what the research is expected to achieve: supplying linguistic criteria for improved understanding of all language phenomena and for facilitating the translation of the Bible into as many languages—no matter how small and how 'insignificant' they may be—as is possible.

Hence, being co-authors is no rarity among the members of the SIL, as it seems best suited to their desire for meaningful personal interaction.

3. *On Donald A. Burquest*

Dr. Burquest is a specialist in theoretical linguistics, with a concentration on African languages and ethnolinguistics. He became a member of the SIL in 1964. In the years 1964, 1966, and 1970 he taught SIL Summer courses at the University of Oklahoma on *Introductory Phonetics* and *Introduction to Linguistics*. From 1968 to 1975 he was affiliated with the Ahmadu Bello University, in Zaria, Nigeria, as a Research Fellow. For five years during that time he worked as primary translator of the New Testament into Angas, a language of the Chadic group, comprised of numerous languages, including Kotoko, Sokoro, and Mubi, which have only a small number of native speakers and of which no written records exist. Most scholars assume that Chadic is a branch of the Hamito-Semitic language family. This research activity resulted in a number of publications, including his Ph.D. thesis of 1973, *A Grammar of Angas.*

While African studies continued to remain a primary sphere of his interest, Burquest moved on to the University of Texas at Arlington, TX in 1975 to pursue an academic career. He teaches mainly graduate courses on a large variety of topics, covering the full spectrum from theoretical linguistics courses—*Linguistic Analysis, Phonological Theory, Grammatical Theory, Universals of Language*—to language aquisition and language teaching—*Child Language Acquisition, Methodology for Teaching English as a Second Language*—as well as subjects dealing with the content side of language such as *Language and Cognition, Semantics,* and *Lexicology.* The courses he has taught on *Swahili Language Structure* and *African Language Structures* illustrate his abiding strong involvement with the continent where he has conducted linguistic field work for seven years.

Teaching and guiding students in their research figure prominently in his overall activities. This is attested, for instance, by two nominations for Teaching Awards in 1994 and the large number of theses, both Ph.D. and M.A., which he has directed over the years.

He undertook extensive travels—within the United States, to Canada, South America, Africa, and to Asia—conducting seminars, directing workshops, and presenting lectures. A small selection should indicate the wide range of topics which he has at his disposal:

(1) *Evidence for an AfroAsiatic Prefix in Angas* (Lecture, University of California, 1977).

(2) *Language, Identity, and Community Development* (Lecture in

Mérida, Mexico, 1978).

(3) *A Proposal for Semantic Projection Rules* (Lecture, Texas Woman's University, Denton, TX, 1978).

(4) *Folklore and Cultural Values* (Lecture, in Lomalinda, Colombia, 1978).

(5) *Shibboleths of Adolescence: Language and Identity* (Lecture, Toronto, 1982).

(6) *Transformational Grammar as an Aid to Fieldwork* (Lecture, San Antonio, TX, 1982).

(7) Directing *Workshop on Gur Languages* (Bobo-Dioulasso, Upper Volta [now Burkina Faso], 1983).

(8) *Recent Developments in Generative Phonology* (Two-day Seminar conducted at Hasanuddin University, Ujung Pandang, Sulawesi, Indonesia, 1990).

(9) Directing *Workshop on Languages of Maluku* at Pattimura University, Ambon, Maluku, Indonesia, 1990).

The published research amply corroborates the impression formed from assessing the public lectures, with the observation to be added that Dr. Burquest shows remarkable achievements also in the field of editing. Apart from several editions of segments in periodicals and collections of research papers, he was also co-editor of the joint publication in linguistics by the University of Texas at Arlington and the SIL from 1991 to 1993. Since then he has assumed the responsibilities of the editor.

4. *On Carol V. McKinney*

Dr. McKinney's university training was in anthropology (B. A., M. A., Ph. D.) and linguistics (M. A.). She also took courses in religious education at the Biblical Seminary (now New York Theological Seminary), New York.

She became a member of the SIL in 1959 and taught SIL courses on *Phonetics* and *Phonology* at the University of Oklahoma in the summers of 1961, 1962, and 1972. She spent almost ten years doing linguistic and anthropological fieldwork overseas:

(1) From 1967 to 1976 (with a one-year interruption), together with her husband Dr. Norris McKinney, she investigated the Bajju (Kaje) language in Nigeria, West Africa. One of the results was the translation of the New Testament into Jju [= Bajju]. According to Grimes (1992:316-354), there are currently 427 languages spoken in Nigeria, a country of 88 million inhabitants. With approximately 300,000 speakers, Kaje is one of the larger languages in the country.

(2) In 1980 she spent five weeks in the Republic of Guinea to do

phonological research on Tyapi, together with other dialects, such as Landoma, a subgroup of Mel languages.

(3)   She spent 1983/84 in Nigeria, doing field research for her Ph. D. thesis on the Bajju language and was affiliated with Ahmadu Bello University, in Zaria, Nigeria, as a Research Associate.

(4)   In 1992 she went for 3½ weeks to Limuru and Nairobi, Kenya, participating in, and contributing to, an SIL *African Area Anthropology Consultants Training Seminar*.

She served at various universities teaching courses on a variety of linguistics subjects, for instance:

(1)   At the University of Michigan teaching *Phonetics* (1960-61).

(2)   At the English Language Institute of the same University she taught *English Pronunciation to Foreign Students* (1964).

(3)   At various times (1976-77, 1978-79, 1980, and 1982) she taught courses on *Phonetics, Linguistic Field Methods*, and a Seminar on *Sub-Saharan Africa* at the International Linguistics Center, the coursework being accredited through the University of Texas at Arlington.

(4)   She taught *Cultural Anthropology* at the Southern Methodist University (1980-81).

(5)   As a staff member of the University of Texas at Arlington from 1986 to 1994 she taught regular courses, e.g., on *Sub-Saharan African Ethnology, Cultural Anthropology*, and *Field Perspectives on Cultural Anthropology* as well as Conference Courses on *Anthropological Field Methods,* on the language of *Akan of Ghana,* on *Nilo-Saharan Linguistics* (with emphasis on Kalenjin, "consisting of three languages: Nandi, Suk [...] and Tatoga" [cf. Greenberg in Sebeok 1971:431], spoken in Kenya).

(6)   During the summers of 1987, 1988, 1990, and 1991 she taught courses on *Anthropological Perspectives for Field Linguists* at the University of Oregon.

Between 1988 and 1994 she served on ten M.A. Thesis and Thesis Substitute Committees at the University of Texas at Arlington.

She read papers on African languages at various professional conferences in the United States and lectured at the *African Orientation Courses* in Zaria, Nigeria, in 1970 and 1971. Lectures in *Perspectives in World Christian Missions Courses* were given in Austin, TX and Wichita, KA, Houston, TX and College Station, TX in 1989 and 1990.

Dr. McKinney's publications dwell mainly on African languages, with the focus on linguistic (1979, 1983, 1993) as well as on anthropological (1976, 1985, 1992) and religious phenomena (1985, 1986, 1994). It is obvious that the three areas cannot, and should not, be kept neatly apart, the less so as the overall objective is apparently to present a comprehensive picture of what major forces are at work in shaping the cultural fabric of a given speech community.

5. *On Gary F. Simons*

Dr. Simons became a member of the Wycliffe Bible Translators and the Summer Institute of Linguistics in 1975. During the same year he served as teaching assistant to Kenneth L. Pike at the SIL in Norman, OK. He obtained his M. A. (1976) and Ph. D. (1979) degrees from Cornell University, in the second instance with a major in General Linguistics and minoring in Computer Science and Classics. His interest in languages, especially classical languages, was already established before he entered graduate school in that he chose Greek, German, and Latin as his major subjects on the B. A. level.

For 1½ years he conducted field work in Papua New Guinea and Solomon Islands, with Joseph Grimes as principal investigator, in the *Language Variation and Limits to Communication Project*. He subsequently continued his involvement with the Solomon Islands by serving, from 1979 to 1983, as Translation Advisor to North Malaita. His translation of the New Testament into Lau, of Solomon Islands, undertaken together with three associates, appeared in 1992, a monumental volume of 863 pages.

Apart from translation work, his great specialty is to provide assistance for "Doing Linguistics in the Computer Age", a frequently used title for his workshops. He does it in three essential ways:

(1) He publishes books (cf., e.g., Simons 1984a, Simons and Thomson 1988, Simons and Kew 1989) and articles (cf., e.g., Simons 1977b, 1980a, 1983a-b, 1989).

(2) He conducts workshops, courses, and seminars, both in the United States and abroad, for instance: Workshop on *Computer Literacy for Social Scientists* (Goroka, Papua New Guinea, December 1983); Workshop on *Computer Literacy for Linguistic Consultants* (Denver, CO, January 1985); Workshop on *Doing Linguistics in the Computer Age* (Ukarumpa, Papua New Guinea, 1-18 June; Honiara, Solomon Islands, 6-15 July; Port Vila, Vanuatu [= New Hebrides], 20-31 July, 1987; Kara, Togo, 9-21, 1989). Workshop on *Academic Computing in SIL* (Ukarumpa, Papua New Guinea, 4-15 February, 1991). Conference course on *Computational Morphology* (University of Texas at Arlington, Fall term, 1994).

(3) Last not least: He has held and still holds important positions, administrative or academic or both, which enable him to help determine significantly the course of action in the field of computer-and-linguistics interaction at the institutions he serves, for instance:

1982-	International Linguistics Consultant, SIL
1984-86	Manager, Language Data Processing, SIL, Dallas, TX
1984-	Editor, *Occasional Publications in Academic Computing*, SIL, Dallas, TX (18 numbers through 1994)
1985-	Adjunct Asst. Prof. of Linguistics, University of Texas at Arlington
1986-	Director, Academic Computing, SIL, Dallas, TX
1989-94	International Text Encoding Initiative, Member of Committee on Text Analysis and Interpretation.

There are other areas where he has developed expertise, but they all involve a strong component of linguistics or computer science or both.

6. *On this Publication*

The book consists of three articles, each one co-authored by Dr. Pike and one of his associates. The first, "Toward the Historical Reconstruction of Matrix Patterns in Morphology," leads into the field of historical linguistics and expands on explorations which Pike has undertaken previously concerning lexical items. The authors now focus on morphological structures by meticulously establishing a comprehensive theory on the basis of several languages. The procedure enriches and solidifies what is currently available in the field of morphological reconstruction.

The second article, entitled "Understanding Misunderstanding as Cross-Cultural Emic Clash," familiarizes the reader with the crucially important role played by language in dealing with the numerous problems encountered in contacts of people from divergent cultural backgrounds. It provides a learning experience based on thorough research into areas of importance for a more general public no less than for the subject matter specialist.

The third article, "The Importance of Purposive Behavior in Text Analysis," takes its lead from the assumption that all "human behavior is purposive". Accordingly, a linguistic text analysis requires the identification of factors that transcend what is immediately given in the text. Even in a fictional text reality is referred to; hence no valid and complete text analysis can afford to neglect the far-reaching exploration of the vital factors of reality and determine their relationship to what is actually expressed in the text.

The authors present a novel approach as to how text analysis can become more relevant as well as more interesting and enjoyable both for the seasoned expert and for the enthusiastic novice in the field.

REFERENCES

Alatis, James E. 1993. "Presentation of the Dean's Medal to Kenneth L. Pike," in *Georgetown University Round Table on Languages and Linguistics 1992*. Edited by James E. Alatis, 4-5. Washington, DC: Georgetown University Press.

Brend, Ruth M. (ed.). 1972. *Kenneth L. Pike: Selected Writings: To Commemorate the 60th Birthday of Kenneth Lee Pike*. The Hague: Mouton.

————. 1987. *Kenneth Lee Pike Bibliography*. Bloomington, IN: Eurolingua.

Brend, Ruth M. and Kenneth L. Pike (eds.). 1976. *Tagmemics*. The Hague: Mouton.

Brend, Ruth M. and Kenneth L. Pike. 1977. *The Summer Institute of Linguistics: Its Works and Contributions*. The Hague: Mouton.

Burquest, Donald A. 1973. *A Grammar of Angas*. Ann Arbor, MI: University Microfilms.

————. 1984. "A Fieldguide for Transformational Syntax." *Innovations in Linguistics Education* 3:2.1-152.

————. 1986. "The Pronominal Systems of Some Chadic Languages." In Ursula Wiesemann (ed.), *Pronominal Systems*, 71-101. Series Continuum 5. Edited by Hansjakob Seiler. Tübingen: Gunter Narr Verlag.

Burquest, Donald A. and Jerold A. Edmondson. 1992. *A Survey of Linguistic Theories*. Dallas, TX: Summer Institute of Linguistics.

Burquest, Donald A. and David L. Payne. 1993. *Phonological Analysis: A Functional Approach*. Dallas, TX: Summer Institute of Linguistics.

Cook, Walter A. 1969. *Introduction to Tagmemic Analysis*. New York: Holt, Rinehart and Winston.

Cowan, William et al. (eds). 1986. *New Perspectives in Language, Culture, and Personality: Proceedings of the Edward Sapir Centenary Conference (Ottawa, 1-3 October 1984)*. Amsterdam and Philadelphia: John Benjamins.

Grimes, Barbara F. (ed.). 1992[1951]. *Ethnologue: Languages of the World*. 12th ed. Dallas, TX: Summer Institute of Linguistics.

Joos, Martin (ed.). 1962. *Readings in Linguistics*. New York: American Council of Learned Societies.

Kaye, Alan S. 1994. "An Interview with Kenneth Pike." *Current Anthropology* 35:3 (June).291-298.

Makkai, Adam (ed.). 1983. "Tribute to Kenneth L. Pike." *Languages for Peace* 1.1-33.

McKinney, Carol V. 1976. "Cultural Change and its Relation to Literacy." *Missiology* IV:1.65-74.

————. 1979. "Plural Verb Roots in Kaje." *Afrika und Übersee*

LXII:2.107-117.

—————. 1983. "A Linguistic Shift in Kaje, Kagoro, and Katab Kinship Terminology." *Ethnology* XXII.281-293.

—————. 1985. *The Bajju of Central Nigeria: A Case Study of Religious and Social Change*. Southern Methodist University: Ph.D. Dissertation.

—————. 1986. "Retention of Traditional Religious Beliefs by Bajju Christians." *Notes on Anthropology*, Special Issue 1.58-66.

—————. 1992. "Wives and Sisters: Bajju Marital Patter*ns*." *Ethnology* XXXI:3.279-290.

—————. 1993. *Globe Trotting in Sandals: A Field Guide to Cultural Research*. 2nd Preliminary Edition.

—————. 1994. "Conversion to Christianity: A Bajju Case Study." Missiology XXII:2.147-165.

Pike, Eunice V. 1981. *Ken Pike: Scholar and Christian*. Dallas, TX: Summer Institute of Linguistics.

Pike, Kenneth L. 1941. *A Reconstruction of Phonetic Theory*. University of Michigan: Ph.D. Dissertation.

—————. 1943. *Phonetics: A Critical Analysis of Phonetic Theory and a Technic for the Practical Description of Sounds*. Ann Arbor, MI: University of Michigan Press.

—————. 1947. *Phonemics: A Technique for Reducing Languages to Writing*. Ann Arbor, MI: University of Michigan Press.

—————. 1948. *Tone Languages: A Technique for Determining the Number and Type of Pitch Contrasts in a Language. With Studies in Tonemic Substitution and Fusion*. Ann Arbor, MI: University of Michigan Press.

—————. 1951. "The Problems of Unwritten Languages in Education." *Report in the UNESCO Meeting of Experts in the Use of the Vernacular Languages*. Paris: UNESCO.

—————. 1955a. *Language in Relation to a Unified Theory of the Structure of Human Behavior*. Part I (Part II, 1955, enlarged 1960; 2nd rev. ed. The Hague: Mouton, 1967). Glendale, CA: Summer Institute of Linguistics.

—————. 1955b. "Meaning and Hypostasis." *Monograph* 8.134-141. Washington, DC: Georgetown University, Institute of Languages and Linguistics.

—————. 1957. "Language and Life: A Training Device for Translation and Practice." *Bibliotheca Sacra* 114.347-362.

—————. 1958. "On Tagmemes, née Gramemes." *International Journal of American Linguistics* 24.273-278.

—————. 1962. *With Heart and Mind: A Personal Synthesis of Scholarship and Devotion*. Grand Rapids, MI: William B. Eerdmans.

————. 1964. "Beyond the Sentence." *Journal of the Conference on College Composition and Communication* 15.129-135.

————. 1965. "Language – Where Science and Poetry Meet." *College English* 26.283-292.

————. 1966a. "A Guide to Publications Related to Tagmemic Theory." *Current Trends in Linguistics* 3. Edited by A. Sebeok, 365-394. The Hague: Mouton.

————. 1966b. *Tagmemic and Matrix Linguistics Applied to Selected African Languages.* Washington, DC: U.S. Office of Education.

————. 1967a. "Grammar as Wave." *Monograph* 20.1-14. Washington, DC: Georgetown University, Institute of Languages and Linguistics.

————. 1967b. *Stir–Change–Create: Poems and Essays in Contemporary Mood for Concerned Students.* Grand Rapids, MI: William B. Eerdmans.

————. 1971. "Crucial Questions in the Development of Tagmemics: The Sixties and the Seventies." *Monograph* 24.79-98. Washington, DC: Georgetown University, Institute of Languages and Linguistics.

————. 1976. "A Poem on Disconnecting Form and Meaning." *Linguistic and Literary Studies in Honor of Archibald A. Hill.* Vol. I: General and Theoretical Linguistics. Edited by Mohammad Ali Jazayery et al., 233-234. Lisse, The Netherlands: The Peter de Ridder Press.

————. 1982. *Linguistic Concepts: An Introduction to Tagmemics.* Lincoln: University of Nebraska Press.

————. 1983. "Towards the Linguistic Analysis of One's Own Poems." *The Tenth LACUS Forum 1983*, 117-128. Columbia, SC: Hornbeam Press.

————. 1985. "Static, Dynamic, and Relational Perspectives Suggested in Words and Phrases." *Scientific and Humanistic Dimensions of Language: Festschrift for Robert Lado.* Edited by Kurt R. Jankowsky, 447-452. Amsterdam: John Benjamins.

————. 1987. "The Relation of Language to the World." *International Journal of Dravidian Linguistics* 16.77-98.

————. 1988. "Bridging Language Learning, Language Analysis, and Poetry, via Experimental Syntax." In Deborah Tannen (ed.), *Linguistics in Context: Connecting Observation and Understanding,* 221-245. Norwood, NJ: Ablex Publishing Corporation.

————. 1993. *Talk, Thought, and Thing: The Emic Road Toward Conscious Knowledge.* Dalias, TX: Summer Institute of Linguistics.

————. 1995a. *Pike's Poems.* [About 600 so far unpublished poems, forthcoming.]

————. 1995b. "Tagmemics in Retrospect: A Biased Personal View." *Papers Presented at the Presession on the History of Linguistics at the*

Georgetown University Round Table on Languages and Linguistics, Tuesday, March 7, 1995, 101-108. Edited by Kurt R. Jankowsky (forthcoming).

Pike, Kenneth L., Hubert M. English, and Alan B. Howes. 1964. *Tagmemics: The Study of Units beyond the Sentence.* Chicago: National Council of Teachers of English.

Pike, Kenneth L. and Evelyn G. Pike. 1977. *Grammatical Analysis.* Dallas, TX: Summer Institute of Linguistics and University of Texas at Arlington. (2nd ed., 1982.)

Pike, Kenneth L. and Evelyn G. Pike. 1983. *Text and Tagmeme.* Norwood, NJ: Ablex Publishing Company.

Pike, Kenneth L. and Gary F. Simons. 1993. "Towards the Historical Reconstruction of Matrix Patterns in Morphology." Published in Russian, in *Voprosy Jazykoznanija* (Moscow) 1.22-44.

Pike, Kenneth L. and Hugh Steven. 1989. *Pike's Perspectives: An Anthology of Thought, Insight, and Moral Purpose.* Langley, British Columbia: Credo Publishing Corporation.

Robbins, Frank, 1995. "The Scope of Research and Field Work of the Summer Institute of Linguistics." *Papers Presented at the Presession on the History of Linguistics at the Georgetown University Round Table on Languages and Linguistics, Tuesday, March 7, 1995*, 57-62. Edited by Kurt R. Jankowsky (forthcoming).

Sebeok, Thomas A. (ed.). 1971. *Current Trends in Linguistics.* Volume 7: *Linguistics in Sub-Saharan Africa.* The Hague: Mouton.

Simons, Gary F. 1977a. "A Dialect Survey of Santa Cruz Island." *Working Papers for the Language Variation and Limits to Communication Project* [= *WPLVLCP*] No. 3. Cornell University: Dept. of Modern Languages and Linguistics.

—————. 1977b. "A Package of Computer Programs for the Analysis of Language Survey Word Lists." *WPLVLCP* No. 7.

—————. 1979. *Language Variation and Limits to Communication.* Ithaca, NY: Dept. of Modern Languages and Linguistics. Repr., Dallas, TX: Summer Institute of Linguistics, 1984.

—————. 1980a. "The Impact of On-site Computing on Field Linguistics." *Notes on Linguistics* 16.7-26.

—————. 1980b. "A Survey of Reading Ability among the To'abaita Speakers of Malaita." *'O'o: Journal of Solomon Islands Studies* 1.43-70.

—————. 1982. "Word Taboo and Comparative Austronesian Linguistics." *Pacific Linguistics* C-76.157-226.

—————. 1983a. "Working Papers on Academic Computing in SIL: Systems Development." *Notes on Computing* 1.15-25.

—————. 1983b. "Working Papers on Academic Computing in SIL:

Software Development." *Notes on Computing* 1.27-40.

——————. 1984a. *Powerful Ideas for Text Processing: An Introduction to Computer Programming with the PTP Language*. Dallas, TX: Summer Institute of Linguistics.

——————. 1984b. "The Lectionary Approach in Scripture Translation." *The Bible Translator* 35:2.216-223.

——————. 1989. "The Computational Complexity of Writing Systems." *The Fifteenth LACUS Forum 1988*, 538-553. Lake Bluff, IL: Linguistic Association of Canada and the United States.

——————. 1991. "The Role of Philosophy in Decision Making." In Gloria E. Kindell (ed.), *Proceedings of the Summer Institute of Linguistics International Language Assessment Conference*. Horsley Green, 23-31 May 1989, 33-42. Dallas, TX: Summer Institute of Linguistics.

Simons, Gary F., Aloysius Jack, Steven Doty, and Ben Kirio (transl.). 1992. *Na Faarongolaa Diana* [The New Testament in Lau, Solomon Islands]. Suva, Fiji: The Bible Society in the South Pacific.

Simons, Gary F. and Priscilla M. Kew (eds.). 1989. *Laptop Publishing for the Field Linguist: An Approach Based on Microsoft Word*. [= Occasional Publications in Academic Computing, No. 14.] Dullas, TX: Summer Institute of Linguistics.

Simons, Gary F. and Linda Simons. 1977. "A Vocabulary of Biliau, an Austronesian Language of New Guinea, with Notes on its Development from Proto Oceanic." *WPLVLCP* No. 2.

Simons, Gary F. and John V. Thomson. 1988. *How to Use IT: A Guide to Interlinear Text Processing on the Macintosh*. Edmonds, WA: Linguist's Software.

Swadesh, Morris. 1934. "The Phonemic Principle." *Language* 10.117-129. Reprinted in Joos 1963:32-37.

Trager, George L. 1943. Review of Kenneth L. Pike, *Phonetics: A Critical Analysis of Phonetic Theory and a Technic for the Practical Description of Sounds* (Ann Arbor, MI: University of Michigan Press, 1943). *Studies in Linguistics* 2:1.16-20.

Wallis, Ethel E. and Mary A. Bennett. 1959. *Two Thousand Tongues to Go: The Story of the Wycliffe Bible Translators*. New York: Harper & Bros.

Wares, Alan Campbell. 1974. *Bibliography of the Summer Institute of Linguistics, 1935-1972*. Huntington Beach, CA: Summer Institute of Linguistics.

——————. 1986. *Supplement to the Bibliography of the Summer Institute of Linguistics (to December 1985)*. Dallas, TX: Summer Institute of Linguistics.

Weiss, Lowell. 1995. "Speaking in Tongues." *The Atlantic Monthly* 275:6 (June).36-43.

TOWARD THE HISTORICAL RECONSTRUCTION OF MATRIX PATTERNS IN MORPHOLOGY

KENNETH L. PIKE AND GARY F. SIMONS
Summer Institute of Linguistics
University of Texas at Arlington

1. *Introduction*

This paper presents a new procedure for historical reconstruction of morphology. In addition to proposing a set of procedures, it illustrates them with examples from a number of languages and elucidates the principles which underlie the procedures. A similar attempt to specify steps in classical historical reconstruction of lexical items was made by Pike (1951, expanded 1957). More recently, Costello (1983) has attempted to develop an approach to syntactic change and reconstruction based on Pike's (1967b) tagmemic approach to language.

What, then, are the basic principles and procedures which need to be added to historical linguistics to better handle morphological reconstruction? In Pike's work (1959, 1982a:19-38), a particular language event can be seen as a particle, or it can be seen as a wave, or it can be seen as a point in a field pattern. As a nonlinguistic illustration of this concept, consider a house. It can be looked at as if it were a single "particle" (or thing), such as might be available for purchase for a certain amount of money; or it can be studied in relation to its current state in the "wave" (or progression) of time, as being almost completed or in good condition or falling down in decay; or it can be looked at from the point of view of its position in a "field" (or neighborhood) of other buildings, such as having neighboring houses on both sides and across the street or as being by itself at the end of a cul-de-sac or being near the grocery store.

From this kind of perspective, we look at classical historical linguistic reconstructions as building on a particle perspective. The linguist is there trying to reconstruct particular units of sound and lexicon over the millennia. The wave perspective enters in as well when sound changes are explained by conditioning environments in the stream of speech.

But it is the field perspective that concerns us here. Field can be seen as pattern, and pattern involves not mere units, and not mere sequence, but intersecting components in an underlying n-dimensional space of the language structure. It is our belief that such patterns can be exploited in the historical reconstruction of language. This paper explains how we propose to do so.

A classical phonetic chart is an example of a field approach applied to sounds. A traditional paradigm of conjugated word forms is a familiar example from morphology. Even in syntax such two-dimensional tables have been used to show how constructions that vary in orthogonal dimensions relate to each other (Pike 1962). In previous work, Pike has defined a generalization of such charts, paradigms, and tables which he takes to be the basic unit of the field perspective; he calls it the *matrix* (Pike 1957, 1962: 243).

When applied to morphology (which is the focus of this paper), a matrix has rows and columns labeled by different sets of semantic functions. The cells at the intersection of rows and columns are filled by phonologically-written grammatical entities, which could be morphemes or morpheme complexes or even submorphemic (but recurring) bits of phonological form. We use the term *formative* as a cover term for the phonological material entered into a cell of a matrix. When a particular formative occurs in every cell of a row or column, it may be called a *vector formative*. A *partial vector formative* occurs when a formative is present in some, but not all, of the cells of a row or column. When multiple vectors (whether complete or partial or both) for the same formative overlap or adjoin, they comprise a *formative block*. As languages change, various formative block shapes can develop over time. The uniqueness of those shapes, in relation to the semantic functions they correlate with, implies that the discovery of comparable formative blocks across languages is not a historical accident but is the result of a shared history that can be reconstructed.

This implies that historical reconstruction of formative blocks may be an important possibility for future comparative-historical work. In this paper we try to illustrate this possibility with examples from various languages. We begin with material from Fore (Papua New Guinea), where Pike (1963) got his initial insight about the field perspective in morphology. We continue with some startling formative block shapes in Algonquian languages, building particularly on the work of Pike and Erickson (1964), using data from Hockett (1948). Then we turn to an example from the Malaitan languages of the Solomon Islands, taken from Simons (1980).

We assume that readers will be more interested in the theoretical underpinning of the procedures, and in the actual methodology utilizing these procedures, than in extensive specific language data. We have, therefore, tried to put into the forefront of our paper statements of the methodology, in the form of numbered procedures, and statements of basic underlying presuppositions, in the form of numbered principles.

Note, in the bibliography, that the big bulk of this work on matrix descriptive analysis, with its underlying implications for historical morphological matrix reconstruction, was published in the 1960's. We hope that now, in the 1990's, the time has come for further historical application of this material. But the basic breakthrough—from our perspective—for using matrix material for historical reconstruction of morphology (versus for description of clause systems, Pike 1962) came as a by-product of a descriptive problem in analyzing, with Scott, the morphology of Fore (Pike 1963, Scott 1978).

2. *Procedures for the Reconstruction of Morphological Matrices*

We now present our procedures for historical reconstruction in the form of a sequence of numbered steps. These should be taken as an initial suggestion, rather than as a complete and final word. The procedures are first described as they are applied to material from Fore and Gahuku of the Eastern Highlands Province of Papua New Guinea. In the second subsection they are further illustrated by application to the Algonquian language family of North America.

2.1 *As Applied to Fore and Gahuku of Papua New Guinea*

The analysis begins by permuting a selected matrix to find an optimal display.

PROCEDURE 1: Permute the rows and columns of a morphological matrix until as many formatives as possible are brought together into contiguous blocks.

One such permutation of object prefixes in Fore (from Pike 1963:2) is given in Figure 1. The startling element in this matrix is the vowel /a/ (which is underlined in the figure to highlight it). It appears both in the row for singular and in the column for first person. Therefore /a/ cannot be simply a morpheme for singular, nor a morpheme for first person. Other interesting formative blocks appear as well. The /si/ is clearly dual—and therefore we put it at the bottom of the chart to separate it off somewhat from the rest of the material. But, in addition, the /t/ clearly helps identify both plural and dual, provided that it is simultaneously either first or second person. In addition, the /n/ clearly forces an interpretation of singular first person, as /k/ does for singular second person. This leaves a zero formative element in the empty consonantal position as identifying third person.

	1st	2nd	3rd
singular	n<u>a</u>-	k<u>a</u>-	<u>a</u>-
plural	t<u>a</u>-	ti-	i-
dual	t<u>a</u>si-	tisi-	isi-

Figure 1: Fore object prefixes (after Pike 1963:2)

Note that in classical terms, it is awkward to call /a/ a morpheme here, because of its function as either singular or as first person—two different vector formatives. Conversely, it is awkward to call /ta/ a single morpheme of first plural, because of its obvious composition of two parts. *Classical morpheme procedures are inadequate here*—and continue to be inadequate as applied, for instance, to English. No extensive morphemic analysis of English has yet covered adequately the result of rapid fusions. For instance, what are the morphemes in /jinjoyit/ "Did you enjoy it?" Analysis by matrix formatives may help in the synchronic study of wave results like this that are currently perplexing when studied through static particle procedures. "Morpheme" might ultimately need redefinition in static, dynamic, and relational terms for different purposes.

PROCEDURE 2: Mark matrix formative blocks to show clearly both the specific components of the total matrix space and the overlapping chunks of that matrix structure.

Figure 2 shows the result of applying the second procedure to the Fore material. The /a/ formative is indicated by the L-shaped block combining the top row and the left column. The dotted square block to the lower left encloses the four items which have /t/, while the solid square to the lower right indicates items with /i/. The /si/ formative is included in the thin rectangular box at the bottom. The dotted rectangle to the right encloses the zero formative for third person. The /n/ and /k/ each represent a partial redundancy; like /a/ they indicate singular number, but they further distinguish the contrast between first person and second person.

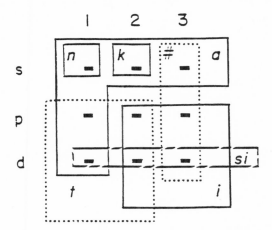

Figure 2: Field structure of Fore object prefixes (from Pike 1963:6)

This kind of representation allows one to see contrastive formative blocks as intersecting chunks of matrix space, rather than as sequential affixes only. (One can call these, if one wishes, "distorted Venn diagrams" for the interlocking semantic structural features of that paradigm.) That is, the presence of a phoneme or a phoneme sequence from this matrix does not by itself guarantee that we know precisely what it means. For example, it takes the intersection of /t/ with /a/ and the absence of /si/ for us to know that we are dealing with first person plural.

PROCEDURE 3: If the matrix structure involves overlapping formative blocks, decide on segmentation breaks between formatives and
pull the single complex matrix structure apart into a sequence of
simple matrices in which there are no overlapping formative blocks.

Figure 3 shows the result of applying the third procedure to the Fore matrix in Figure 2. We see that a sequence of three matrices is needed in order to pull apart the overlapping formative blocks. When performing this procedure the analyst is very likely to face indeterminacies in the attempt to segment the formatives. This does not pose a problem for the method as explained below in section 4 (see principles 10 through 12).

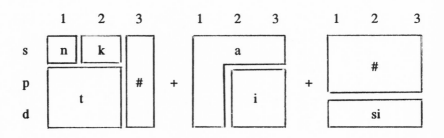

Figure 3: Fore object prefix as three simple matrices of nonoverlapping
          formative blocks

PROCEDURE 4: Compare similar permutations of related paradigms
in the language to look for internal reconstruction of the shape of
formative blocks which are persistent across matrices, even in the
face of radically modified phonological material.

Note now the subject suffixes of Fore, given in Figure 4. In this matrix, there is a striking subset of formative structures in which /n/ crisscrosses from first person plural to second person singular; while /w/ crisscrosses from first person singular to second and third person plural. These formatives are capitalized and underlined, respectively, in the figure in order to highlight the crisscross pattern. (Note that there is no permutation that can put the /n/ formatives in adjacent cells; at best they must crisscross in this diagonal pattern.)

	1st	2nd	3rd
singular	-u<u>w</u>	-aaN	-ay
plural	-uN	-aa<u>w</u>	-aa<u>w</u>
dual	-us	-aas	-aas

Figure 4: Fore subject suffixes (after Pike 1963:8)

When one adds an emphatic suffix to the morphological material in Figure 4, the fusion leaves morpheme identity very obscure, as in Figure 5. But still, "point by point they have the same internal pattern, in spite of different formatives" (Pike 1963:11), that is, Figure 5 retains the formative shape of Figure 4, in spite of the added material for emphasis. Note in particular how the crisscrossing shape is preserved (again highlighted by means of capitalization and underlining). First person plural and second person singular share the same formative (namely, /mpe/); while first person singular shares the same formative (namely, zero) with second and third person plural.

	1st	2nd	3rd
singular	-o<u>#</u>	-aaMPE	-ami
plural	-oMPE	-aa<u>#</u>	-aa<u>#</u>
dual	-ome	-aame	-aane

Figure 5: Fore subject suffixes fused with an emphatic suffix (after Pike 1963:9)

Once a distinctive pattern like this has been recognized, one searches for other instances of comparable structures. It is our experience that a language tends to use a particular kind of matrix pattern more than once throughout its structure.

PROCEDURE 5: Make comparable descriptive matrix studies of a number of other languages which are assumed to be related to the first.

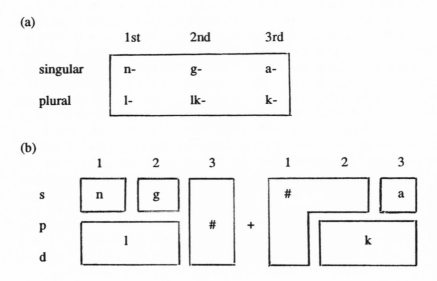

Figure 6: Object prefixes of Gahuku: (a) as a matrix of complex forms, (b) as a sequence of formative matrices

Another description of material in Papua New Guinea, carrying further the kind of analysis given above for Fore, is found in Deibler (1964, 1973, 1976) for the Gahuku language. Wurm (1982:124) treats Gahuku and Fore as belonging to two different subfamilies of the East-Central family of the East New Guinea Highlands stock of Papuan languages. Figure 6 displays the object prefixes matrix of Gahuku (Deibler 1976:14) which corresponds to the Fore matrix in Figures 1 through 3. Part (a) of the figure gives the matrix of full forms. Part (b) pulls these apart into a sequence of formative matrices (following Procedure 3). Note that the dual versus plural distinction, which is neutralized in Gahuku in the object prefixes while being preserved in the subject suffixes, is represented in these formative matrices in order to maximize their congruence with the corresponding matrices of Fore.

> PROCEDURE 6: Take a matrix structure found in one of the languages and check to see if a similar structure can be found in one or more of the other languages. If so, try to guess at a reconstructed matrix shape from which all of these can be derived.

In comparing the matrices of Figures 1 and 6(a) we can see some similarities between the morphemes, but it is not until we factor out the formatives and compare the formative block structures (as in Figures 3 and 6(b)) that the high degree of correspondence between the prefixes in the two languages stands out. Note that the formative structure of the first matrix is identical in both languages. Furthermore, all of the phonological forms have the same point of articulation; the only differences are in the manner of articulation of two of them. The second matrix is much the same as well. The distinctive L-shaped pattern of the /a/ formative in Fore is preserved in Gahuku; it is just that the phonological content has been deleted in every cell except the 3rd person singular (where it could not be deleted without losing the prefix altogether since that cell has zero in the first matrix). The most intriguing result is that the /i/ formative of Fore ends up corresponding to the /k/ formative of Gahuku. We would need to appeal to evidence from other languages to find a plausible explanation for that. Finally, note that the neutralization of the dual versus plural distinction in Gahuku results from the loss of the dual morpheme (which explains the absence of the third formative matrix evidenced by Fore in Figure 3).

	1st	2nd	3rd
singular	-uve	-ane	-ive
plural	-une	-ave	-ave
dual	-usive	-asive	-asive

Figure 7: Gahuku subject suffixes (from Deibler 1976:24)

As a further example, Figure 7 gives the Gahuku subject suffix matrix which corresponds to the Fore material given in Figure 4. The two parts of Figure 8 give a direct comparison of the formative structures across the two languages. The first formative matrix in both languages is virtually identical. The third matrix in Gahuku preserves the distinctive crisscross pattern found in the second matrix in Fore; in fact, the second matrix in Fore looks very much like a fusion of the second and third matrices in Gahuku. Note, too, that the second matrix in Gahuku which contains only the /si/ formative for dual is exactly the same as the matrix which appeared in the Fore object prefix (Figure 3) but was absent in the corresponding Gahuku prefix (Figure 6).

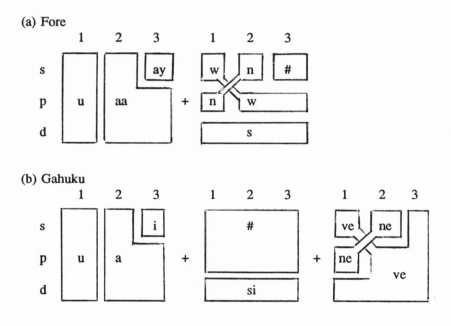

Figure 8: Formative matrices for subject suffixes of Fore and Gahuku

We will not go so far at this point as to propose a reconstruction of these matrices for Proto Eastern Highlands; we have not yet performed the detailed comparison with other languages of the family. However, the correspondences of patterns are so striking and the likelihood that they could be due to independent development is so low, that we are confident that these matrix patterns are retained from the parent language and could be reconstructed straightforwardly. (Compare the similar statement by Ivanov (1977:20) regarding syntactic reconstruction: "The relation of the same categories to the same surface structures cannot be accidental and makes the exact syntactical reconstruction possible.") These examples show that matrix patterns can be widely retained across languages separated by significant genetic distance. Deibler has in fact suggested to Simons (personal communication, quoting Simons 1980:14) that formal correspondences of this nature may prove a better criterion for classifying this group of languages than lexical correspondences, which are often rarer.

PROCEDURE 7: Try to reconstruct the phonological component of each formative block of the reconstructed matrix structure. Make use of the traditional comparative method for this (see, for instance, Pike 1951, Hoenigswald 1960, and Weinreich, Labov, and Herzog 1968). Note, however, that the fusion which is prevalent in morphological matrices is likely to distort the regular sound changes attested in content morphemes.

Having not made a reconstruction of matrix shape in the previous step, we cannot attempt the phonological reconstruction. This step of the procedure is illustrated below with material from other language families. The topic of fusion and its impact on sound change is covered at length below in sections 3 and 4.

2.2 *As Applied to Algonquian Languages of North America*

Object

		1	2	3	4	12	1p	2p	3p
	1		k-	n-	n-			k-	n-
	2	k-		k-	k-		k-		k-
	3	n-	k-		w-	k-	n-	k-	
Subject	4	n-	k-	w-		k-	n-	k-	w-
	12		k-	k-					k-
	1p		k-	n-	n-			k-	n-
	2p	k-		k-	k-		k-		k-
	3p	n-	k-		w-	k-	n-	k-	

Figure 9: Potawatomi person prefixes for the transitive animate independent verb (after Pike and Erickson 1964:202)

We now turn to one of the most astonishing applications of the descriptive use of formative blocks—its application to the transitive animate verb affixes in Potawatomi, an Algonquian language of North America. The data are taken from Hockett (1948) by Erickson, as reported in Pike and Erickson (1964).

Figure 9 charts a transitive animate verb prefix, which is made up either of /k-/ or /n-/ or /w-/. The matrix is arranged with rows reflecting the person and number of the subject and columns reflecting the person and number of the object. Singulars are given before plurals. An additional person beyond first, second and third person is here called fourth person; and first person plural inclusive is given as "12". Note that the phoneme forms—for example /k-/—seem to be scattered "wildly" throughout.

We now permute the rows and columns of the matrix to bring the formatives together into contiguous blocks (Procedure 1). It turns out that if we move the row for second person to the top, followed by the row for second plural (2p) immediately below it, along with inclusive (12) immediately below that, and ordering the columns similarly as 2, 2p, 12, then the /k-/ elements form a contiguous block in the top three rows and in the leftmost three columns. Similarly, moving the row and column for first plural next to first singular shows a further grouping, with the /n-/ elements grouped together in rows and columns to the lower right of /k-/. The /w-/ elements then end up grouped further to the lower right. The resulting formative blocks are then marked off (Procedure 2), as shown in Figure 10. (Since these prefixes contain only a single formative, Procedure 3 does not apply in this case.) We call the result an L-shaped matrix, because of the way the shapes of the formative blocks go "around the corner." (In other permutations of the matrix, the ranking pattern shows up as an intersection of horizontal versus vertical formative vectors in a cross pattern, as illustrated on page 203 of Pike and Erickson 1964. Ranking is more easily perceived by us when charted in the L-shape, but the other arrangement is sometimes necessary for conflation with other parts of the same construct, as on their page 207.)

Figure 10 implies that whenever the second person is involved, whether as the subject or as the object, the prefix /k-/ is used. On the other hand, if second person is not involved, but first person is, then the /n-/ occurs in that slot. But if neither second nor first person is involved in the action, so that only third and fourth person are involved, then /w-/ is used. The gaps along the diagonal are in some sense reflexive; second person subject occurring with second person object is not signaled by /k-/; nor are first or third person reflexives signaled.

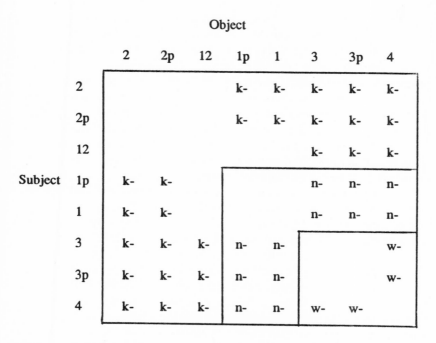

Figure 10: Potawatomi person prefix matrix permuted to show ranking structure (after Pike and Erickson 1964:203)

Notice that this implies a basic fact about languages: an L-shaped matrix implies that the item in the largest L-pattern outranks other items in the matrix. The implication here for Potawatomi is that there is a ranking such that if both a second person and a non-second person referent are involved in the verb, then the second person referent will be signaled by /k-/, regardless of whether it is subject or object; the person of the outranked referent must be shown elsewhere in the verb. Also, further structures must be used to signal whether the /k-/ represents the subject or the object (which here is indeterminate). This ranking structure can be startling for scholars who for generations have assumed—with little discussion of the assumption, so far as we have seen—that first person is "obviously" expected to outrank second person (perhaps because we count 1-2-3, not 2-1-3). (For a radically different type of ranking that involves intersecting matrices in three dimensions, see DuBois, Upton, and Pike 1980.)

If the reader wishes to see how such a Potawatomi prefix in fact fits into a full verb, with its various suffixes (which function, among other things, to identify the person and number of the second-ranking participant and to

identify which participant is subject and which is object), see the chart in
Pike and Erickson (1964:208-209) or the detail in Hockett (1948:142, 144).
For comparison to other kinds of verbs and nouns in Potawatomi, see
Erickson (1965). It turns out that ranking structures recur throughout
Potawatomi, both in relation to several suffix positions in the independent
transitive animate verb, and to some extent in other verb types and even in
nominal types. This provides scope for the internal reconstruction of such
ranking structures (Procedure 4).

We turn now to the historical reconstruction of ranking patterns in Proto
Algonquian. The descriptive listing of comparative matrix shapes (Procedure
5) has been done by Morgan (1966) for eight Algonquian languages. Figure
11 reproduces his matrices for the prefix charted in Figure 10. (Unfortu-
nately, he failed to include the first person plural inclusive forms.)

Fox

Object

		2s	2p	1s	1p	3s	3p	4
	2s			ke	ke	ke	ke	
	2p			ke	ke	ke	ke	
	1s	ke	ke			ne	ne	
Subject	1p	ke	ke			ne	ne	
	3s	ke	ke	ne	ne			φ
	3p	ke	ke	ne	ne			φ
	4					φ	φ	

Cree

Object

		2s	2p	1s	1p	3s	3p	4
	2s			ki	ki	ki	ki	
	2p			ki	ki	ki	ki	
	1s	ki	ki			ni	ni	
Subject	1p	ki	ki			ni	ni	
	3s	ki	ki	ni	ni			φ
	3p	ki	ki	ni	ni			φ
	4					φ	φ	

Ojibwa

Object

		2s	2p	1s	1p	3s	3p	4
	2s			ki	ki	ki	ki	
	2p			ki	ki	ki	ki	
	1s	ki	ki			ni	ni	
Subject	1p	ki	ki			ni	ni	
	3s	ki	ki	ni	ni			o
	3p	ki		ni	ni			o
	4					o	o	

Potawatomi

Object

		2s	2p	1s	1p	3s	3p	4
	2s			k	k	k	k	k
	2p			k	k	k	k	k
	1s	k	k			n	n	n
Subject	1p	k	k			n	n	n
	3s	k	k	n	n			w
	3p	k	k	n	n			w
	4	k	k	n	n	w	w	

Shawnee

Object

		2s	2p	1s	1p	3s	3p	4s	4p
	2s			ki	ki	ki	ki		
	2p			ki	ki	ki	ki		
	1s	ki	ki			ni	ni		
Subject	1p	ki	ki			ni	ni		
	3s	ki	ki	ni	ni			ho	ho
	3p	ki	ki	ni	ni			ho	ho
	4s					ho	ho		
	4p					ho	ho		

Delaware

Object

	2s	2p	1s	1p	3s	3p	4
2s			kə	kə	kə	kə	
2p			kə	kə	kə	kə	
1s	kə	kə			nə	nə	
1p	kə	kə			nə	nə	
3s	kə	kə	nə	nə			wə
3p	kə	kə	nə	nə			wə
4					wə		

Subject (row label for Delaware)

Cheyenne

Object

	2s	2p	1s	1p	3s	3p	4
2s			ne	ne	ne	ne	
2p			ne	ne	ne	ne	
1s	ne	ne			na	na	
1p	ne	ne			na	na	
3s	ne	ne	na	na			ʔe
3p	ne	ne	na	na			ʔe
4s					ʔe	ʔe	
4p					ʔe	ʔe	

Subject (row label for Cheyenne)

Blackfoot

Object

		2s	2p	1s	1p	3s	3p	4s	4p
	2s			kit	kit	kit	kit		
	2p			kit	kit	kit	kit		
	1s	kit	kit			nit	nit		
Subject	1p	kit	kit			nit	nit		
	3s	kit	kit	nit	nit			φ	φ
	3p	kit	kit	nit	nit			φ	φ
	4s					φ	φ		
	4p					φ	φ		

Figure 11: Matrix structure for person-number prefix in eight Algonquian
languages (from Morgan 1966:5-6)

Note in Figure 11 that the ranking shapes are unchanged across all eight
languages. These similarities are too regular and too complex to be attri-
buted to borrowing or independent development. Thus we do not hesitate
to posit an identical ranking structure for the parent matrix in the proto language (Procedure 6), even though some of the cognate formative blocks
have as disparate phonological content as Cheyenne /ne-/ versus Blackfoot
/kit-/.

Reconstructing the phonological form for each formative block of the
proto matrix is not as straightforward since they differ somewhat across
languages. Where Potawatomi has /k-/, Fox has /ke-/, Cree, Ojibwa, and
Shawnee have /ki-/, Delaware has /kə-/, Blackfoot has /kit-/, and Cheyenne
has /ne-/. Similarly, where Potawatomi has /n-/, Fox has /ne-/, Cree, Ojibwa,
and Shawnee have /ni-/, Blackfoot has /nit-/, Delaware has /nə-/, and
Cheyenne has /na-/. For Potawatomi /w-/, Delaware has /wə-/, Ojibwa has
/o-/, Shawnee has /ho-/, Cheyenne has /'e-/, and Fox, Cree, and Blackfoot
have zero.

Phonological reconstruction has been done in some detail for Algonquian. Note, for example, early reconstruction of the Proto Algonquian sound system in Bloomfield (1946); Goddard (1979) provides a more recent treatment. Goddard (1967 and 1974) has also attempted an extensive treatment of Algonquian verbs with reconstructions. We thus defer to his scholarship in positing the phonological content of the proto formative blocks as *ke-, *ne-, and *we- (Procedure 7). The resulting reconstructed matrix is given in Figure 12.

Object

		2	2p	12	1p	1	3	3p	4
	2				*ke-	*ke-	*ke-	*ke-	*ke-
	2p				*ke-	*ke-	*ke-	*ke-	*ke-
	12						*ke-	*ke-	*ke-
Subject	1p	*ke-	*ke-				*ne-	*ne-	*ne-
	1	*ke-	*ke-				*ne-	*ne-	*ne-
	3	*ke-	*ke-	*ke-	*ne-	*ne-			*we-
	3p	*ke-	*ke-	*ke-	*ne-	*ne-			*we-
	4	*ke-	*ke-	*ke-	*ne-	*ne-	*we-	*we-	

Figure 12: The reconstructed matrix for the person-number prefix of Proto Algonquian transitive animate verbs

The full marking of the Algonquian transitive animate verb to disambiguate the person and number of subject and object involves the conflation of the above prefix matrix with the matrices for three suffixes, as shown in Pike and Erickson (1964:207) and Morgan (1966). The other three matrices can be reconstructed following the same procedure to achieve a full reconstruction of the transitive animate verb morphology. (Since doing so here would not add appreciably to the explanation of the methodology, that step is left as an exercise for the reader.)

3. *Principles of Language Change in Morphological Matrices*
The matrix perspective affords us new insights into the nature of language change. Traditional comparative linguistics speaks of split and merger

(as of phonemes or of words) as the primary mechanisms of historical change. The matrix perspective highlights two other mechanisms, namely, fusion and analogy, which seem to play a very important role in morphological (as opposed to purely phonological or lexical) change. These principles are introduced in section 3.1 and then illustrated with data from Malaita, Solomon Islands, in section 3.2.

3.1 *Basic Matrix Types and Basic Mechanisms of Change*

Pike (1963:16 and 1965:204) has described two basic matrix types; these are illustrated in Figure 13. The first, which he calls a *simple* matrix, has a full vector formative for each row and column of the matrix. That is, the first row contains the same morpheme all the way across carrying the meaning of that row; the second and third rows have different morphemes representing their respective meanings. Likewise, each column has its own morpheme carrying the meaning of that column. Each cell of that matrix, therefore, contains two morphemes—one representing the meaning of the row, and the other representing the meaning of the intersecting column. The left side of Figure 13 represents this simple shape.

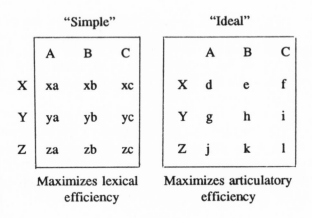

Figure 13: Two regular paradigm types

The second basic matrix pattern, which Pike calls an *ideal* matrix, has only one formative per cell of the matrix. Every cell thus has a different formative which simultaneously signals the meaning of the row and the column. The right side of Figure 13 represents this ideal shape.

With these definitions of the two fundamental matrix types in place, we are now in a position to state our basic principles of morphological change.

The first two principles define the significance of the two major mechanisms of morphological change:

Principle 1: Phonological fusion can lead away from a simple matrix of vector formatives toward an ideal matrix with single-celled formatives.

Conversely,

Principle 2: Paradigmatic analogy can lead away from an ideal matrix of single-celled formatives toward a simple matrix with vector formatives.

Fusion, coming from rapid speech, can merge the two morphemes of a cell into one phonological element with the combined semantic meanings. This kind of fusion is a normal phonological process in rapid speech, with no accompanying loss of intelligibility in the immediate context of a conversation. As such fusion progresses over time and becomes frozen, the two original vector formatives in each cell of the matrix can become one single-celled formative.

But pressure can be brought to bear in the opposite direction as well. By a process of analogy, similar phonological bits in single-celled formatives can be reinterpreted as partial vector formatives and ultimately extended to cover the whole vector, thus leading to new conventional morphemes.

The pressure to change by fusion or to change by analogy is not strictly arbitrary, for as Pike (1965:205) points out:

Principle 3: The two basic matrix shapes embody efficiencies of different kinds. A simple matrix is maximally efficient in requiring the lowest number of morphemes to signal all the distinctions in the matrix, while an ideal matrix is maximally efficient in requiring the shortest utterance to signal each distinction.

Fusion and analogy can then be interpreted as processes which change a matrix (or at least one cell of a matrix at a time) from one efficiency type to the other. Fusion leads to greater articulatory efficiency by making the phonological material in a matrix cell shorter and easier to pronounce. Analogy, on the other hand, leads to greater lexical efficiency by reducing the number of morphemes in the lexicon.

The matrix perspective thus leads us to the following explanation of something that students of language change have recognized for over a century:

Principle 4: The history of language is characterized by a perpetual oscillation between two opposite tendencies, the tendency toward greater articulatory efficiency versus the tendency toward greater lexical efficiency.

The first part of this statement of principle is almost a direct quote from Hermann Paul (1889, section 307); the second part is our reinterpretation of what the opposing tendencies are. Pike (1965:206) has observed further, that "presumably the stability of human language reflects this kind of oscillation, about an indeterminate norm, with unknown limits, and perhaps seldom reaching the limits of the fully regular types."

Another way of looking at phonological fusion is to view it as a process of entropy. If such a process should continue indefinitely, many morphological structures of the simple type would disappear, and communication could eventually be damaged. In order to counter this physical tendency in pronunciation, so as to preserve communicative possibility, some kind of counter-process must also be involved, or we would have no languages at all. Loss of communicative clarity, through fusion, can be re-established by a process of analogy which re-establishes simple matrices. More recently, Pike has referred to this counter-process as anti-entropy (in Headland, Pike, and Harris 1990:42-44). Note the similarity of this formulation to that of Paul (1889, section 367): "Each disorganization is followed by a reorganization," through "analogical formation" after the "devastation of sound change."

The matrix perspective can also subsume the notion of "borrowing" as a mechanism of language change. Where different speech communities are in contact, we can view dialect as one more dimension of the typical speaker's field structures. Borrowing can then be interpreted as change via analogic extension along this dimension of dialect (Simons 1980:16).

3.2 *As Illustrated by Malaitan Languages of Solomon Islands*

We now illustrate these principles of change via fusion and analogy with an example from the morphological reconstruction of Austronesian languages of the Solomon Islands, specifically a reconstruction of the pronoun system of the languages spoken on the island of Malaita. For this, we take material from an unpublished manuscript by Simons (1980).

Following procedures like those we have presented in section 2, Simons has reconstructed a system of pronouns for Proto Malaitan which has four numbers (singular, dual, trial, and plural), four persons (first exclusive, first inclusive, second, and third), and many functional classes (including free pronouns, possessive suffixes, object suffixes, and multiple categories of subject markers). As a basis for the example given here, Figure 14 shows the forms reconstructed (using the above methodology) for the free pronouns and the future subject markers in singular and dual numbers.

	Free pronoun	Future subject marker
1 sg	*nau	*kukai
2 sg	*'oe	*'okoi
3 sg	*nia	*kai
1in dl	*gurua	*gurua kai
1ex dl	*gamirua	*mirua kai
2 dl	*gamurua	*murua kai
3 dl	*girarua	*girarua kai

Figure 14: Some pronoun forms reconstructed for Proto Malaitan (from Simons 1980:46)

Inspection of Figure 14 indicates a proto system that is somewhere between the two extremes of maximal articulatory efficiency and maximal lexical efficiency. For instance, the future subject markers show a common formative, namely /*kai/, with the exception of a vowel assimilation in the second person singular form indicating the beginnings of fusion. Note, too, that the basic pattern for the future subject markers is that the /*kai/ formative is added to a form very much like the free form. There are a number of significant differences from the free forms, however, which lessen the lexical efficiency in favor of greater articulatory efficiency.

Twelve languages are spoken on Malaita, an island only 100 miles long and 20 miles wide at its widest point. Two of these languages, To'aba'ita and Fataleka, which are spoken just 20 miles apart and share 72% cognates on the Swadesh 100-word list, exhibit radically different historical developments, in terms of the principles we have been discussing. One of them, To'aba'ita (see L. Simons 1986 for a synchronic description of the pronouns), has employed fusion throughout to produce a pronoun system that approaches maximum articulatory efficiency. For instance, in the future subject markers, the dual forms which involve eight to ten phonemes each in the reconstructed forms are fused to forms of only four phonemes. On the other hand, Fataleka has employed analogy throughout to produce a pronoun system that approaches maximum lexical efficiency. For instance, to form the future subject markers, the /kai/ formative has been extended to apply to every future form, while the free pronouns have been extended to be the basis (without change) of the future forms. The result is that the To'aba'ita lexicon must record every future subject marker as a unique form, while the Fataleka lexicon need record only the single form /kai/ and the syntactic fact that it is combined with the free pronoun. Figure 15 illustrates these developments.

	To'aba'ita	Proto Malaitan	Fataleka
	FutSubMrk	FutSubMrk	(Free Form) FutSubMrk
1sg	kwai	*kukai	(nau) kai
2sg	'oki	*'okoi	('oe) kai
3sg	kai	*kai	(nia) kai
dl 1 in	koki <— Via Fusion	*garua kai Via Analogy —>	(koro) kai
dl 1 ex	meki	*mirua kai	(karo) kai
dl 2	moki	*murua kai	(kamoro) kai
dl 3	keki	*girarua kai	(keroa) kai

←MAXIMUM ARTICULATORY EFFICIENCY   MAXIMUM LEXICAL EFFICIENCY→

Figure 15: Morphological change via fusion versus analogy in future subject markers of two Malaitan languages (after Simons 1980:45)

The example of fusion in To'aba'ita is quite striking from the standpoint that Proto Malaitan forms have been reduced to half their original length without any loss of information. Figure 16 shows this process for two of the future subject markers. The Proto Malaitan forms consist of four morphemes totaling eight phonemes in length. The Pre-To'aba'ita stage shown in the figure represents an intermediate proto language common to all the languages of the north Malaitan subgroup. In the contemporary To'aba'ita forms, we see that the fusion process has left a single phoneme as a vestige of each of the original morphemes.

	2nd dual	2nd trial
Proto Malaitan	*mu-rua ka-i	*mu-oluka-i
Pre-To'aba'ita	*mu-ro ka-i	*mu-lu ka-i
To'aba'ita	m - o- k- i	m - u -k -i

Figure 16: Fusion in the development of To'aba'ita future subject markers
(after Simons 1980:44)

Figures 17 and 18 illustrate that this fusion has taken place without loss
of information. First, Figure 17 gives a matrix of the dual and trial future
subject markers. Note that the second person forms are the ones given in the
preceding figure. Synchronically, it makes the most sense to analyze these
forms as having two morphemes, the first signaling person and number and
the second signaling their syntactic function as future subject markers. Note
that all eight person and number contrasts are preserved in unique forms for
the first morpheme, though drastically abbreviated in phonological shape
from the Proto Malaitan. The allomorphic variation of the /-ki/ morpheme
in the third person forms is actually a case of a displaced contrast. The two
subject marker forms that would be expected if the second morpheme did
not vary, namely /keki/ and /kiki/, occur in the plural row of the full paradigm. To avoid the potential ambiguity, the vowels of the Pre-To'aba'ita
number morphemes, *-ro and *-lu (see Figure 16), have ended up being
inserted into the future-forming suffix to form /-koi/ and /-kui/. This has the
effect of retaining the original number information.

	1in	1ex	2	3
dual	ko-ki	me-ki	mo-ki	ke-koi
trial	ku-ki	mi-ki	mu-ki	ki-kui

Figure 17: Results of fusion in To'aba'ita future subject markers (after
Simons 1980:43)

Figure 18 shows how the person and number morpheme of To'aba'ita developed. In Proto Malaitan, person and number marking was achieved through a simple matrix pattern. In the permutation given in Figure 18, the person distinctions are signaled by column vector formatives and the number distinctions by row vector formatives. This matrix structure is preserved in the Pre-To'aba'itan stage, though all formatives have been abbreviated to a single syllable. In present-day To'aba'ita, the original simple matrix with regular vector formatives has fused completely into an ideal matrix with single-celled formatives. Note that all of the original contrasts are present in the fused matrix, with the number distinctions now preserved in the vowel height while the person distinctions are preserved in the combination of consonant and vowel roundedness.

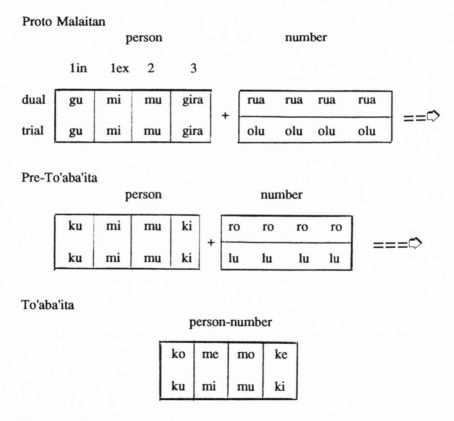

Figure 18: Fusion without loss of information in To'aba'ita person-number formatives (after Simons 1980:44)

On the other hand, just 20 miles from To'aba'ita, the Fataleka language has changed the same proto language material through the process of vector extension by analogy. A full example was given above in Figure 15. Figure 19 takes just the singular forms and illustrates how the third singular form is extended to replace a set of single-celled formatives by a full vector formative.

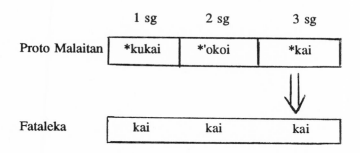

Figure 19: Extension by analogy in Fataleka future subject markers (after Simons 1980:39)

Figure 15 summarizes the strikingly different paths these closely related languages have taken in developing from Proto Malaitan—one opted for syntagmatic fusion to maximize articulatory efficiency while the other opted for paradigmatic analogy to maximize lexical efficiency. That such radical differences could exist between languages geographically so close and lexically so overlapping is one of the most astonishing things we have seen. We are not aware of any other approach to historical linguistics which makes this result appear so "reasonable" when discovered. This example suggests that once the process of vector extension by analogy is well under way, it does not easily revert to morpheme fusion, nor does the reverse appear easily to occur.

4. *Principles that Underlie the Matrix Approach to Reconstruction*

With the principles of language change introduced in section 3 serving as a background, we can now consider some of the general principles which underlie the reconstruction procedures introduced in section 2. These principles, we believe, explain why the reconstruction procedures work. Each of the seven procedures is considered in turn with its underlying principles.

Procedure 1 involves putting the morphological material into a matrix and permuting the rows and columns to discover the inherent matrix structure. Underlying this is the belief that:

Principle 5: The analyst must be prepared to choose a temporary standpoint as an observer, viewing units either as (a) relatively static and with sharp boundaries—a particle view—or (b) points in a temporal sequence of units with identifiable nuclei but with fuzzy borders—a wave view—or (c) points in a larger (e.g., matrix) pattern of semantic relationships—a field view.

The general possibility and value of such observer flexibility is discussed in Pike (1959) and in Pike (1982a:19-38), where it is identified as a fundamental component of universal human nature. This flexibility of observer viewpoint is crucial to the reconstruction methodology presented here.

Pike's original breakthrough on using a matrix perspective in synchronic analysis of morphology came as a result of the inadequacy of a particle view by itself. As he wrote at the time (Pike 1963:10):

Principle 6: A "linear display of allomorphs—though often useful and relevant to and valid within particle theory—is insufficient where [semantic] category and formative fail to coincide neatly."

Our breakthrough in historical reconstruction also comes as a result of recognizing the inadequacy of the particle view by itself. The traditional comparative method is based on a particle view in which reconstructable units are seen as particles which change by shift, split, and merger. We have found that the primary mechanisms of morphological change are, rather, fusion and analogy, for which we need the wave and field perspectives. Thus,

Principle 7: For historical reconstruction one must deal with units like morphemes not only as particles which may change over time by processes like shift or split or merger, but also as units in a wave sequence which may change over time by a process of fusion, and as units in a field structure (or matrix) which may change over time by a process of analogy (via vector extension).

Procedure 2 involves marking the formative blocks in the permuted matrix structure. The existence of formatives which are neither single-celled nor full-vectored suggests the following principle:

Principle 8: The meaning of a morpheme does not have to be in an isomorphic relation between one phonological shape and one semantic contrastive feature, nor a sum of contrastive features always tied to that particular morpheme.

The meaning of a formative, including a classical morpheme as a special instance, may in fact be the disjunction of a set of semantic features (or of combinations of features). The determination of which features are relevant at a particular point in a larger construction depends on the intersection of those sets of meanings for all the formatives in the construction. There must be an analog of a Venn diagram reflecting the overlapping relationships of the potential meanings of various formatives at different places in the structure to force the selection of the particular meanings which are relevant and accessible to the hearer at that particular moment. Thus,

> Principle 9: The total signal as to the components of meaning involved in a particular instance of a constructed form is carried not simply by the addition of meanings of the constituent morphemes, but by the intersection of formative blocks when the matrix structures are conflated.

This process of matrix conflation is illustrated in detail in Pike and Erickson (1964:207).

Procedure 3 involves positing segmentation boundaries between formatives and arranging the segmented formatives in a sequence of matrices. But this is not always easy to do; it is often difficult, if not impossible, to decide where a boundary belongs. Indeed, this result is predicted by the wave perspective:

> Principle 10: In a wave view, units are seen as having identifiable nuclei (at the crests) but as having indeterminate (or fuzzy) borders (in the troughs).

Several decades ago Pike pointed out (1943:107) that a phonetic segment can be defined as a sound "having indefinite borders but with a center that is produced by a crest or trough of stricture." Later he found that comparable indeterminacies could obtain in identifying morpheme breaks as well. (For waves of meaning, see Pike 1982a:120; for phonological waves, see pp. 24-26, 88-91. For waves introduced as an important component in analysis of clause and sentence, see Pike 1967a.)

The wave perspective, as applied to morphological analysis, thus leads to the following procedural principle:

> Principle 11: The analyst must be prepared to accept some indeterminacy—or arbitrariness—in the place where one chooses to divide between contiguous (or even simultaneous) formatives which are to

be entered into the cells of coterminous (or possibly overlapping) matrices.

Pike discovered this principle in his first work with matrices in morphology, namely, in the Fore study cited above in section 2.1. In that study, Scott was forced to make some arbitrary choices (Pike 1963:14-15), but the typical result was that such arbitrariness in segmentation point did not "affect basically the topology of the system—the number of matrices, their cells, and their interrelations," even when the phonetic detail of the formative components was changed within the cells of the system (Pike 1963:15).

A special case of segmentation indeterminacy occurs when the formatives involve overlap, either partially or completely. Historical reconstruction of some languages will be hindered if one expects words and sentences to be reconstructed as simple sequences of simple phonemes. Some scholars in Asia, for instance, have objected to the "Euro-centered" view that begins with phonemes; they would rather treat the syllable as the basis for reconstruction. Denlinger (1987:19-23) points out that in Sino-Tibetan languages, the syllable is the unit that bears tone, as well as other simultaneously articulated contrastive features like length, nasalization, and laryngeal voice quality. He also notes that it is more productive to analyze syllables not as a sequence of phonemes but as consisting of an "initial" plus a "final" (or rhyme) in which individual phonetic features (such as nasal versus stop) play a role in making key contrasts. In a matrix reconstruction, the relevant simultaneous formatives (such as tone, length, nasalization, voice quality, or distinctive features) would be pulled apart into separate matrices for comparison. (For a synchronic analysis of tone using matrix techniques, see Pike and Jacobs 1968, Pike 1970:81-83, and Pike 1982b. Pike and Becker (1964) treat vowel quality, length, and tone in Navaho verbal inflections.)

The danger of being misled by an errant segmentation decision in comparative reconstruction is even less than in a synchronic study. This is because comparing the same material across languages makes it possible to detect and unravel the fusions that may obscure the original segmentation and thus complicate the synchronic picture for a given language. This leads to a further procedural principle:

Principle 12: The analyst must be prepared to go back and change early segmentation decisions as the comparative data from related languages bring insight about fusions that have taken place.

Comparison of data from related languages brings such insight because,

Principle 13: Syntagmatic fusion of sounds, or phonological abbreviation of morphemes, often occurs with no loss of original contrastive lexical units, because of preservation of vestiges in later stages.

This point is illustrated in detail in section 3.2 with the data from Malaita. See Figures 16 and 18 above.

A final note on segmentation indeterminacy is an early observation by Pike which may help explain why comparativists (and linguists in general) have favored a particle view of language over a wave view (Pike 1963:15):

> Principle 14: "It is not [necessarily] communicative value which is impaired by the segmentation indeterminacy, but [sometimes it is] only the convenience of the particle analyst who wishes to proceed from morpheme to word to sentence (or the reverse) in clean-cut steps."

Procedure 4 involves comparing different matrix structures within the same language to see what is possible in terms of an internal reconstruction of an earlier stage of the language. A principle that underlies this procedure is the recognition that,

> Principle 15: A language tends to utilize a particular kind of matrix pattern more than once throughout its structure.

When a given structure recurs throughout the language, internal reconstruction can posit its existence at an earlier stage of the language. We have already illustrated above in section 2 the recurrence of the crisscrossing pattern in Fore and of the L-shaped pattern in Potawatomi. In fact, in the latter case, the L-shaped pattern is so pervasive that it occurs in different permutations in different matrices.

Another principle that is useful in internal reconstruction is the following:

> Principle 16: When one finds a more-or-less regular formative system, a break in the regularity of that system may imply a change over time.

That is, if a matrix is essentially of the simple type (with mostly vector formatives), then one should check to see if fusion can explain the exceptions to the regular pattern, making it plausible to reconstruct a simple matrix. On the other hand, if the matrix is essentially ideal (with mostly single-celled formatives), then one should check to see if analogic extension can explain the exceptions to the regular pattern, making it plausible to reconstruct an ideal matrix. In external reconstruction, one would not rely solely on such inferences, but would look for evidence from other languages to support a posited reconstruction. Such reasoning can still be useful, however, in developing hypotheses to test with external data. (For an example of matrix techniques applied to a problem in internal reconstruction, see Pike and Becker 1964.)

Procedure 5 involves making comparable matrix studies in related languages in order to find evidence for an external reconstruction of an earlier stage of the language. The basic principle which underlies this quest for the reconstruction of matrices is:

Principle 17: Matrix formative patterns may be retained over time, in spite of heavy fusion which may conceal (in the early stages of research) the historical continuation of common phonological sources.

And following from this is the further principle of reconstruction that:

Principle 18: Shared matrix formative patterns, especially distinctive ones, are more likely to be there because of historical preservation, than because of arbitrary independent development.

Some years ago Pike was in Germany showing to Professor Hansjakob Seiler, a linguistic historian, the Fore crisscrossing structure (see Figures 4 and 5 above). This prompted him to observe that he had found the preservation of a similar crisscross pattern in a submatrix of the nominal inflection system of Classical Greek. That is (quoting him from Pike 1965:208n): "this submatrix has become, in the course of development towards Post-classical and Modern Greek, the basis of the whole nominal inflection" (with references given there to his publication on the subject). This was the first strong support, from a historian, of the assumption that matrix pattern could in fact contribute toward historical reconstruction of morphology.

Procedure 6 involves attempting to reconstruct matrix structures by comparing them across languages. The suggestion to reconstruct shapes of formative blocks before attempting to reconstruct their phonological content is based on the following principle:

Principle 19: Matrix formative shapes are often more consistently retained than the phonological content of those formatives.

We believe this to be the case because of the following:

Principle 20: Affixes and other grammatical morphemes which are short and unstressed are particularly susceptible to fusion and other forms of irregular change over time.

Note that the traditional comparative method for reconstruction works best on lexical roots. From a wave perspective, such forms (which normally bear stress) occur in the flow of speech at the crests of the waves; in this most salient position of the wave they are most likely to follow laws of regular sound change. Unstressed grammatical morphemes, however, occurring in the troughs of the waves (in the regions of fuzziness between the clear centers) are not as susceptible to follow the postulated sound laws and are much more likely to change in irregular ways. We therefore believe that,

Principle 21: In reconstructing morphology, matrix reconstruction is often more certain than phonological or morphemic reconstruction.

Reconstructing the structure of a matrix works because the elements being reconstructed are emic units of a language. That is,

Principle 22: A matrix formative block, having both a form and a meaning, is an emic unit of pattern; as such it is susceptible to reconstruction.

As an emic unit, a formative block is also "well-defined as to contrast, [etic] variation, and distribution" (Pike 1963:11) and may be described in these terms.

In classical comparative linguistics, we look for correspondences between emic units in which a similarity of form correlates with a similarity of meaning. One contribution of the matrix approach to reconstruction is that the shapes of the formative blocks give a formal characterization (and visualization) of the meaning of the emic units involved. As a result, the shapes of the blocks can be quickly and easily compared to discover the degree of meaning similarity between potentially corresponding units.

Procedure 7 involves attempting to reconstruct the phonological content of the formative blocks. In reconstructing these phonological forms, the analyst should take advantage of the traditional comparative method and use regular sound change as much as possible to explain differences in phonological forms between languages. However, because of principle 20 above, the regular sound laws cannot be expected to work for affixes to the same extent that they do for root morphemes. Thus,

Principle 23: In the absence of regular sound changes, the phonological content of a matrix formative can be reconstructed by positing a form which (1) leads to the attested daughter forms by applying
plausible phonological changes, and (2) offers the most parsimonious
set of changes possible that produce the attested forms.

Because of the effect described in principle 20 and the widespread tendency
toward greater articulatory efficiency described in principle 3, phonological
changes like assimilation, coalescence, weakening, and deletion, though irregular from the standpoint of historical sound laws, are nevertheless plausible
and to be expected. The factor of parsimony is a time-honored evaluation
criterion in historical linguistics; in the case of competing reconstructions,
the one which requires the fewest independent changes is generally pre-
ferred.

The notion of phonetic rank of stricture, developed by Eunice Pike
(1954, also summarized in K. Pike 1967b:329-331), may be helpful in explaining changes like weakening and deletion. She proposes ranking the
phonemes of a language in a number of dimensions (such as degree of stricture of the oral cavity), and shows in a comparative study of Mazatec dialects in Mexico, that it is consonants of lower rank which are typically deleted in sound change. Extensive discussion of strength hierarchy can also
be found in Hooper (1976, especially pp. 196-205).

5. *Summary*

Numerous articles on matrix analysis were published by Pike and colleagues in the 1960's. These articles pointed out the potential contribution
of a matrix approach for identifying historical morphological relationships
between languages and for understanding processes of change in morphological systems. They opened the door to the development of an approach
to historical reconstruction of morphology based on comparison of matrices.

In this article we have attempted to describe such an approach. The key
to the approach lies in viewing the units to be compared and reconstructed
not simply as particles in isolation, but also as points in waves of temporal
sequence and as points in fields of semantic relationships.

The traditional comparative method for lexical reconstruction focuses on
units as particles which shift, split, and merge over time. The proposed
matrix method for morphological reconstruction focuses on units (namely,
matrix formative blocks) as points in waves and fields. As points in waves,
these units are seen to change by a process of syntagmatic fusion. As points
in fields, they are seen to change by a process of paradigmatic analogy. A
fundamental tension between greater articulatory efficiency on the one hand,
versus greater lexical efficiency on the other, keeps both mechanisms of

change active in morphological systems. It is our hope that these insights based on viewing language through wave and field perspectives will augment the particle-based contributions of 19th century linguistic historians to offer a richer comparative method that is effective for historical reconstruction in morphology.

REFERENCES

Bloomfield, Leonard. 1946. "Algonquian." *Linguistic Structures of Native America, Viking Fund Publications in Anthropology 6*, Harry Hoijer et al. (eds.). New York, NY: The Viking Fund.

Brend, Ruth M. (ed.). 1964. *Advances in Tagmemics*. Amsterdam: North-Holland Publishing Co.

——————— (ed.). 1972. *Kenneth L. Pike: Selected Writings: To Commemorate the 60th Birthday of Kenneth Lee Pike*. The Hague: Mouton.

Costello, John R. 1983. *Syntactic Change and Syntactic Reconstruction: A Tagmemic Approach*. Dallas, TX: The Summer Institute of Linguistics and the University of Texas at Arlington.

Deibler, Ellis W. 1964. "The Application of Matrix to Gahuku Verbs." *Occasional Papers,* Series A, No. 3, Linguistic Circle of Canberra Publications (now Pacific Linguistics) 3.17-26.

———————. 1973. *Gahuku Verb Structure*. Dissertation, University of Michigan.

———————. 1976. *Semantic Relationships of Gahuku Verbs*. Summer Institute of Linguistics Publications in Linguistics, Number 48.

Denlinger, Paul B. 1987. "'Tone' in Sino-Tibetan." In Agatha C. Brankamp, Yi-chin Fu, Arnold Sprenger, and Peter Venne (eds.), *Chinese-Western Encounter: Studies in Linguistics and Literature*, pp. 3-24. Taipei: Chinese Materials Center.

DuBois, Carl D., John Upton, and Kenneth L. Pike. 1980. "Constraints on Complexity Seen via Fused Vectors of an n-Dimensional Semantic Space." *Semiotica* 29.209-243.

Erickson, Barbara. 1965. "Patterns of Person-Number Reference in Potawatomi." *International Journal of American Linguistics* 31.226-236.

Goddard, Ives. 1967. "The Algonquian Independent Indicative." *Contributions to Anthropology and Linguistics* I (Algonquian), pp. 66-106. National Museum of Canada, Bulletin 214.

———————. 1974. "Remarks on the Algonquian Independent Indicative." *International Journal of American Linguistics* 40.317-327.

———————. 1979. "Comparative Algonquian." In Lyle Campbell and Marianne Mithun (eds.), *The Languages of Native America: Historical and*

Comparative Assessment, pp. 70-132. Austin, TX: University of Texas Press.

Headland, Thomas N., Kenneth L. Pike, and Marvin Harris. 1990. *Emics and Etics: A dialogue between Kenneth Pike and Marvin Harris*. Newberg Park, CA: Sage Publications.

Hockett, Charles F. 1948. "Potawatomi I: Phonemics, Morphophonemics, and Morphological Survey." II: "Derivation, Personal Prefix, and Noun." III: "The Verb Complex." IV: "Particles and Sample Texts." *International Journal of American Linguistics* 14.1-10, 63-73, 139-149, 213-225.

Hoenigswald, Henry M. 1960. *Language Change and Linguistic Reconstruction*. Chicago, IL: The University of Chicago Press.

Hooper, Joan B. 1976. *An Introduction to Natural Generative Phonology*. New York, NY: Academic Press.

Ivanov, Vyacheslav V. 1977. "The Relation between Different Grammatical Levels in the Linguistic Evolution." *Sprache* 23.20-24.

Morgan, James O. 1966. "A Comparison of the Transitive Animate Verb in Eight Algonquian Languages." *Anthropological Linguistics* 8:5(2). 1-16.

Paul, Hermann. 1889. *Principles of the History of Language*, translated by Herbert A. Strong from the 2nd edition [1886]. New York, NY: Macmillan.

Pike, Eunice V. 1954. "Phonetic Rank and Subordination in Consonant Patterning and Historical Change." *Miscellania Phonetica* 2.25-41.

Pike, Kenneth L. 1943. Phonetics: *A Critical Analysis of Phonetic Theory and a Technic for the Practical Description of Sounds*. Ann Arbor, MI: University of Michigan Press.

————. 1951, amplified 1957. *Axioms and Procedures for Reconstruction in Comparative Linguistics: An Experimental Syllabus*. Santa Ana [now Huntington Beach], CA: Summer Institute of Linguistics.

————. 1959. "Language as Particle, Wave, and Field." *The Texas Quarterly* 2.37-57. Reprinted in Brend 1972:129-143.

————. 1962. "Dimensions of Grammatical Constructions." *Language* 38.221-244. Reprinted in Brend 1972:160-185.

————. 1963. "Theoretical Implications of Matrix Permutation in Fore (New Guinea)." *Anthropological Linguistics* 5:8.1-23.

————. 1965. "Non-Linear Order and Anti-Redundancy in German Morphological Matrices." *Zeitschrift für Mundartforschung* 32.193-221.

————. 1967a. "Grammar as Wave." *Monograph* 20.1-14. Georgetown University, Institute of Languages and Linguistics. Reprinted in Brend 1972:231-241.

————. 1967b [1954, 1955, 1960]. *Language in Relation to a Unified*

Theory of the Structure of Human Behavior. The Hague: Mouton and Company.

——————. 1970. *Tagmemic and Matrix Linguistics Applied to Selected African Languages*. Norman, OK: Summer Institute of Linguistics, The University of Oklahoma.

——————. 1982a. *Linguistic Concepts: An Introduction to Tagmemics*. Lincoln, NE: University of Nebraska Press.

——————. 1982b. "Tune and Tone: Generalized Syntagmatic Pitch Patterns Constrained by Particular Lexical Patterns." *Journal of West African Languages* 12:2.2-41.

Pike, Kenneth L. and Alton L. Becker. 1964. "Progressive Neutralization in Dimensions of Navaho Stem Matrices." *International Journal of American Linguistics* 30.144-154.

Pike, Kenneth L. and Barbara Erickson. 1964. "Conflated Field Structures in Potawatomi and in Arabic." *International Journal of American Linguistics* 30.201-212. Reprinted in Brend 1964:135-146.

Pike, Kenneth L. and Jill Jacobs. 1968. "Matrix Permutation as a Heuristic Device in the Analysis of the Bimoba Verb." *Lingua* 21.321-345.

Scott, Graham. 1978. *The Fore Language of Papua New Guinea*. Pacific Linguistics, Series B, No. 47.

Simons, Gary F. 1980. "Morphological Reconstruction and Change in the Pronoun Systems of the Malaitan Languages." A paper presented at the Third New Zealand Linguistics Conference, Auckland, New Zealand, September 3-5, 1980. Unpublished manuscript.

Simons, Linda L. 1986. "The pronouns of To'aba'ita (Solomon Islands)." In Ursula Wiesemann (ed.), *Pronominal Systems*, pp. 21-35. Tübingen: Gunter Narr Verlag.

Weinreich, Uriel, William Labov, and Marvin I. Herzog. 1968. "Empirical Foundations for a Theory of Language Change." In W. P. Lehmann and Y. Malkiel (eds.), *Directions for Historical Linguistics*, pp. 95-180. Austin, TX: University of Texas Press.

Wurm, Stephen A. 1982. *Papuan Languages of Oceania*. Tübingen: Gunter Narr Verlag.

UNDERSTANDING MISUNDERSTANDING AS CROSS-CULTURAL EMIC CLASH

KENNETH L. PIKE AND CAROL V. MCKINNEY
Summer Institute of Linguistics
University of Texas at Arlington

1. *The Observer and Names of Things, Individuals, and Situations are Components of Understanding*

2. *Native Speakers React to Emic Units*

3. *Entities Occur in Part-Whole Hierarchies of Three Types*

4. *Four Universal Underlying Characteristics (Comparable to Four Cells in a Tagmemic Unit) Interlock, but with Clashing Manifestations in Different Cultures*

5. *Oral Societies*

6. *Event Orientation versus Time Orientation*

7. *An Emic View of Truth*

8. *Ethnicity*

9. *Obtaining Useful Emic Advice*

10. *Culture as Particle, Wave, and Field*

11. *Emic Cross-Cultural Understandings and Misunderstandings in Perspective*

Culture and language learning form an essential inseparable dyad for understanding in cross-cultural contexts. In order to avoid misunderstanding and cultural clash—all too common occurrences when working cross-culturally—the individual who seeks to work successfully in a second culture context needs to gain an emic view of that other culture (Headland, Pike, and Harris 1990). In this paper we seek to give some guidance concerning areas that the learner in a second culture context needs to address. We begin by exploring the significance of naming and categorization in language and culture learning, two key areas that can help one avoid cultural misunderstandings and ultimate failure when working cross-culturally.

1. *The Observer and Names of Things, Individuals, and Situations are Components of Understanding*

[a] Until we name something, by word or phrase, we cannot easily refer to it in a way that we can explain to others—or even "recognize" it ourselves in its repeated occurrences with its minor or internal changes. Misunderstandings can occur across two or more cultures, if there are different names for and understandings of a situation. This can occur where the names are not directly or easily translatable from the one language and culture into the other.

It is often helpful to learn the names of persons with whom one has contact. To call people by name or by the appropriate kinship category shows substantial respect for them. For example, among the Bajju in Nigeria, West Africa, where Carol McKinney worked, a woman is known by the name of either her oldest or her youngest child. Carol McKinney was often known to Bajju as "Mama Mark" or "Mama Christy". To so honor a woman by use of this form of address indicates that a woman has status, a status that a single woman or a barren woman does not have.

Contrastively, in some other cultures, e.g., the Mazatec of Mexico, the opposite is true because the name may be used to cause damage to an individual by witchcraft (Eunice Pike, personal communication, Dallas, 1993). In such cultures people may withhold knowledge of their own names from others. If a situation arises where individuals feel they must give their names, in order to avoid or reverse potential damage, they may call themselves by the name of the person they are a bit uneasy about, as for example they have done with Eunice Pike. In so doing they know that if the name were used, it would not be against themselves, but against the other individual. And in Mazatec culture, a mother may use a private name when calling her son, when she would be afraid to have others use his name in the same circumstance.

[b] Categorization of things, with their names, allows us to build our relation to or reaction within the world around us. Deletion of the implicit

reference to the physical world might lead to an untalkeable idealism; deletion of the mental categorization might lead to an unlivable materialism. We need a linking of the two, not as contradictions, but as a livable relation—which we will call here an emic view (see Section 2). Cross-culturally, this may lead to surprises—where we would have assumed that some relations are universally to be expected, but where we may receive surprises and even culture shock. The world and thought must be tied together, but not always in the same way. In such relations, language must join with gestures and actions to form a crucial bridge across cultural differences.

For example, in parts of northern Australia, certain ethnic groups (at least in the past) have not had words for 'right' and 'left'—even though they could describe adequately any geographical situation in which they found themselves (Eunice Pike, personal communication, Dallas, 1993). For instance, as expert trackers they could find lost westerners in the desert! Or when going to a doctor, for example, they might say "My north ear hurts" (assuming, of course, that they were standing facing in a direction appropriate to the statement of the moment). Eunice, the source of these data, on one occasion was walking with a colleague and with a local Australian. Suddenly the aborigine shouted out loudly, "Ssssnake, jump east!" Eunice found it difficult to follow such clear directions!

Categorization of things with their names can be analyzed into taxonomies which identify folk knowledge of people within a specific culture or subculture. We find that folk taxonomies are a cultural universal, though one can expect different categorizations within specific cultures. Kay states that folk taxonomies are "a means of organizing relations of meaning among items in natural languages and cognitive systems" (1971:872). Such analyses move from the general to the specific.

Flora and fauna particularly lend themselves to taxonomic analysis because of their inherent structures. Within a western ethnobiological taxonomy the usual criteria for placing plants, animals, and birds into taxonomies are structural. For example, birds with webbed feet are placed into one category while those without webbed feet fall into another. Be aware that other possible criteria for taxonomic analyses exist within different cultures. For example, the Guahibo in Colombia classify animals according to where they live. One group consists of animals that live on the ground, and another group has animals that live in trees (Kondo 1991:25).

Clues to folk taxonomies in cultures often come from linguistic markers of categories. Lakoff notes that "Classifier languages—languages where nouns are marked as being members of certain categories—are among the richest sources of data that we have concerning the structure of conceptual categories as they are revealed through language" (1987:91). Classifier languages include all of the Bantu languages with their system of noun classes as well as languages in the larger Benue-Congo language family. Denny and Creider (1986) correlate the noun class system of Proto-Bantu with semantic based classification with respect to configurational features, i.e., the shapes of the objects within the classes.

To illustrate, in Jju people fall into the *bə-* noun class as in the following examples:

bənyet	"people"
Bəjju	"Bajju, Kaje"
Bətyap	"Batyap, Kataf"
bəpfong	"workers"
bəyecen	"strangers, foreigners, visitors, guests"

And several foods fall into the *di-* noun class, as for example, *dinam* "meat" and *ditong* "honey". When new loan nouns enter Jju, each must fit into one of the existing noun classes. When first entering a cross-cultural situation with a noun class system, the individual needs to learn each noun class including the types of semantic categorizations that correlate with each noun class.

[c] Within a culture, language helps bridge gaps between perceived reality and thought coming from imagination or from dreams. Language helps to make human action possible, as for example in enabling us to differ from animals in humans' abilities to discuss factors which are not in their immediate environment, such as philosophy, religion, science, or jokes. For example, though a shepherd dog can trace and select sheep in a way that we cannot, it cannot enter into this argumentation. It lacks the names and categorization potential as one component that is necessary for doing so.

[d] In all categorization, units are identified by features which differentiate them (i.e., contrastive features), as well as by features which vary without affecting the identification of the units (free or conditioned variation), and by appropriateness of occurrence (distribution at particular places) in patterns of the language or society or behavior within that society, or by their impact on that behavior, or belief.

For instance, Geertz, an anthropologist, said, "Yet the difference, however unphotographable, between a twitch and wink is vast" (1973:6). Native English speakers recognize these two gestures as being significantly or emically different in their intent and impact.

There are also significant features embedded within categories. In a second illustration of features within categories we note that a baseball game differs from cricket in its rules—it has contrastive features including the way a run is scored; a 'strike' in baseball is made by hitting a ball, or by hitting at it, or by having it pass over the plate in certain places; and a person may come to bat only at certain parts of the game (when it is his team's turn to bat).

Thirdly, we look at variation among the Waorani (Auca) of Ecuador. In their folktales they point out that their ancestors said that "wherever the rainbow stands is the place where the good clay pits are" (Evelyn Pike and Saint 1988:105-106). Following the rainbow, they go to search for clay, and they hope to find it there. Within their folk categorization they must never point at the clay pits or at the rainbow with their hands; they assert that if they do so it would cause their arms to become paralyzed. They must only nod with their heads.

If we only understand the rainbow from a western perspective, we note, as Barfield stated, a rainbow "is the outcome of the sun, the raindrops and your own vision" (1967:15). We know that "if you walked to the place where the rainbow ends, or seems to end, it would certainly not be there". However, this understanding of rainbows and the Waorani understanding differ. To work effectively within the Waorani system of categorization, a part of their worldview, it is important to understand this difference and to work within it.

A classical reference linking observer, language, and perception is found in Kant, who asserted that "We can attain to a knowledge of *appearances* only, never to that of the *things in themselves*" (as quoted in Manthey-Zorn [1938] 1966:70). Goodenough states that "there is good reason for taking a language as my point of departure . . . [in relation to] . . . the content of culture" (1981:vi). Because of this centrality of language in culture learning, in order to really understand another culture the person who desires to work cross-culturally must spend the time, energy, and memorization effort to learn the language of the other culture. Not to do so makes the cross-cultural worker dependent upon others for an understanding of that situation.

The philosopher Searle asserts that "For a large number of social and psychological phenomena the concept that names the phenomenon is itself a constituent of the phenomenon" (1984:78). And Polanyi says that "All human thought comes into existence by grasping the meaning and mastering the use of language" (1969:160). Further, the phenomenologist Gadamer says that "Language is the fundamental mode of operation of our being-in-the-world and the all-embracing form of the constitution of the world" ([1966] 1976:3). And the psychologist Bruner says that "every concept must be defined as much by what it excludes as by what it includes" (1974:42) (cf. contrastive features, above).

2. *Native Speakers React to Emic Units*

[a] People are able to act within or discuss the characteristics of their own native system, following its structured rules, even when the rules are not verbalized by them. They can use the same vocabulary, the same grammar, and the same sounds as others of their culture. Americans can understand the basic vocabulary of baseball (see 1d) and talk about it to some degree, but they would have more difficulty discussing cricket. In the same way, native speakers of English can recognize and mimic easily the words 'pie' versus 'buy', or 'beat' versus 'bit', or 'ban' versus 'band', all of which contain two sounds that are emically different and that differentiate meanings. But speakers of some other languages might have substantial difficulty in trying to mimic the pronunciation of those words, or in hearing the differences between these word pairs. Emic 'native reaction' to data may differ across cultures.

For example, Kenneth Pike had been studying the Mixtec language of Mexico (an Indian group in the highlands of Oaxaca) for some time. One day, however, his Mixtec language teacher decided to try to hear and pronounce an American word. So he asked Pike: "How do you say *cuchi* in your language?" Pike replied: "pig". The native speaker of Mixtec replied, mimicking it as best he could: "wheel". Pike repeated: "pig!!"; the other replied, again: "wheel", and never did much better than that. Why not? The reasons include the following: (1) He had no final consonants in his language, so he could not find one to use for /-g/; but he used, even in Mixtec, a few words from Spanish. One Spanish word he used was *sal* for "salt"—so he used the /-l/ from that, instead of the /-g/. (2) He also had no difference between words such as "beat" and "bit" that English has; so he used the closest sound which he does have, which was the vowel of "wheel". (3) Finally, he had no initial consonants with a puff of breath (as aspiration) after it, as English /p-/ does in "pig"; but he reacted (unconsciously) to the fact that it was made with both lips involved—and he knew a Spanish word which had an aspiration related to (but preceding) a labial sound, as in *juez* (for "judge"—where the "ju-" is pronounced as /hw/); so he used the /hw-/ for that. What incredibly elegant action, with such cross-culturally unintelligible results! Why?

[b] All languages are partly alike, and partly different, and so, also, are nonverbal behavior patterns. As an "absolute" universal, there are sounds of some kind in all languages. All use some kind of vowel action. All have a few consonants. All use some kind of rhythm to pull sounds into groupings in some kind of phonological patterning.

For example, one may expect to find the sound /t/ in any language, or the vowel /a/. One may expect to find syllables with at least one initial consonant and a vowel. But the number of consonants can vary from a very few to a couple of dozen or more; and a syllable may be composed of a single consonant and a vowel, or of four consonants plus one to three vowels plus one to three consonants.

By way of illustration we find that in Jju, a language spoken by the Bajju in Nigeria, West Africa, there is a series of lenis consonants as well as a corresponding series of fortis consonants. The only consonants that do not fit into this fortis-lenis consonant contrast are the double stops (/gb/ and /kp/). The fortis-lenis consonant contrast occurs in such words as *bvón* "goat" and *bvvon* (orthographically the fortis consonant is here represented by bvv) "to be different, v.". Add tone to this fortis-lenis contrast, and one can say *Bvón ə yet bvvon bvòn*, "A goat is different from goats" (note that in the noun class to which *bvon* belongs the difference between singular and plural is marked by a tone contrast). A Jju speaker might use such a sentence in teaching Jju to a non-Jju speaker.

As an absolute universal, people, from every culture which has survived, have had to eat, to sleep, and to have families. Differences between cultures in eating habits, sleeping customs, and types of families are myriad; and for the individual who is seeking to work cross-culturally this may result in misunderstandings and cultural clashes if not understood adequately and appreciated. For example, some people eat snakes, or animals (e.g., cats, dogs, horses, or pigs) which other people leave alone. All people must sleep—but some do so on straw mats, whereas others sleep on soft mattresses. And the placement of an individual sleeping with respect to the door of the house is significant in some cultures. For example, a Bajju man traditionally would not sleep with his head closer to the door than his feet. If he did so, death might come to call him at night, and he would find no escape. Rather he would sleep on his left side, with his bow and arrows near at hand, and with his feet closest to the door, so that if death or an enemy calls, he would be prepared for action.

People in all cultures must find culturally approved ways of dealing with anger and aggression. For example, people in some cultures fight with spears whereas others depend on nuclear weapons as deterrents.

In another example, among the Bajju polygyny is widespread, and this leads to bickering and jealousy among co-wives and their respective children. In fact, the word əW:uk meaning "co-wife" also translates into English as "jealousy" as well as "co-wife". However, in order to keep that jealousy within bounds that allow this polygamous institution to continue there are acceptable means for one co-wife to express her frustrations with her other co-wife or co-wives. Each wife has her turn to cook food for their husband, and on the day it is one wife's turn to cook, while grinding grain for supper she will sing her frustrations against her rival(s). The next day the other co-wife sings in response as she grinds. And children go from compound to compound listening to these grinding songs to hear the latest gossip within various households!

But people are people, in each instance. And brilliance does not depend upon the available tools. One of Pike's analytical helpers among the Mixtec had only been through the fourth grade of elementary school—but (Pike says) "as nearly as I could judge, he was mentally equal to any of my colleagues on the faculty of the University of Michigan, in Ann Arbor. His ability to proofread tone in Mixtec (after he had learned to type!) was much greater than mine."

[c] Both form and meaning are required for human emic units and systems. Part of the reason for this dualism is the fact that the form and meaning can crisscross, in the sense that a single form (e.g., spelling) may represent two or more meanings (words); and a single meaning may be represented by two or more forms (e.g., paraphrase). And across languages, of course, the same pronunciation may represent radically different words.

Suppose, for example, that we have a box divided into squares by transparent dividers. Take a large number of pebbles, and toss them into the big box. They end up in a pattern of squares. But if the starting box has a grid with diagonal dividers, pebbles tossed into it will end up in patterns of diagonal shape. Different languages are like such contrastive grids. The pebbles, metaphorically meaningful words, end up in metaphorical paragraphs the structure of which depends upon the phonological, grammatical, and referential grids of the particular language.

In a second example, again from Jju, we note that the word *ba* can have multiple meanings dependent on placement within a clause. For example, *ba* is the independent subject pronoun meaning "they"; it is also the verb meaning "come". So a good Jju sentence is *Ba ba*, "they came". Two other words that are closely related in sound are *ba'* (ba with a glottal stop following it) indicating negation and *Baba* meaning "father". These two words can further expand possibilities of sentences all of which involve some collocation of the syllable *ba*. For example, we can say *Ba ba ba'*, "They did not come"; and *Baba ə ba*, "Father came"; and *Baba ə ba ba'*, "Father did not come"!

[d] A person (or a nonpersonal thing) may be viewed from different perspectives, but in each case as the same emic unit. It may be seen as a "particle", or as a "wave", or as a "field" (Pike 1959). From a slightly different perspective, the same data may be treated as paradigmatic, syntagmatic, or systemic.

By way of illustration, the growing person, as an entity, may be seen as in motion, i.e., as a wave (with middle life being a nucleus of the wave, perhaps). The individual's relationship to his family and nation shows him as a point in a field. But the person himself is a "particle", viewed as an entity in himself. The person, that is, can be seen in relation to dynamic processes, to group relations, and to identifying features.

In language a syllable like "ran" can be seen as a wave, with the vowel as its nucleus; it can be seen as a field, in that it is part of a whole set of words in a lexicon; and it can be seen as a particle, in that we are talking about it as if it were in fact a "thing" or morpheme isolatable for discussion.

A long time ago Heraclitus said that "Into the same river you could not step twice; for other waters are ever flowing" (fragment 41, in Patrick 1889). From our perspective, however, the river is emically the same (we give it the same name a few minutes later), even though etically the specific waters are in fact different then. Heraclitus, elsewhere, says "Into the same river we can both step and not step" (fragment 81, in Patrick 1889)—reflecting, here, on a relation to our insistence on both emics and etics, but not, of course, called by those terms.

And a piece of music, with four simultaneous parts, may be seen as a field system, with the parts occurring approximately together. The progress on to a climax may be felt as sequential, or syntagmatic. The playing of the same part by different instruments, on different occasions, may be seen as paradigmatic, with the same position in the music being filled by different players.

[e] A "self" (or "soul") may itself be treated as a single unit—defined, in this context, as the nonphysical part of the person, different from the person's physical form. This is a non-mechanistic definition with the self and physical parts interlocking and interacting, but different. (A mechanistic view might treat the self as a viewpoint of the analyst, who abstracts some components of physical form or action or situation for purposes of discussion. The view we present here is a theistic one.) One component of the self, as seen here, is the ability to choose among certain alternatives that are presented to it by the environment and/or its heredity.

By way of illustration, a judge might in a court grant a person the right to drive a bit erratically (etically), so long as he does not hurt anyone, and keeps within legal (emic) boundaries. Yet in some circumstances the driver would be expected to break a legal requirement in order to meet a higher moral emic obligation—the saving of the life of someone who stumbled into the road, but this higher moral obligation could be fulfilled only by having the car cross an "unpermitted" line. Physical, moral, and religious choices can occur within emic cultural hierarchies.

In some Hindu cultures, a different priority may need attention. If by accident one kills a cow with his automobile, he may be in danger of being killed immediately by the bystanders, because of the religious significance of the cow in that culture.

3. *Entities Occur in Part-Whole Hierarchies of Three Types*

Language occurs in physically-arranged emic structures of phonology, in morpheme-arranged emic structures of grammar with its meaningful lexical signals, and in encyclopedic-arranged emic referential structures of the action in relation to background of time or space or knowledge network. Nonverbal behavior has parallel elements of relevance of physical action, as well as physical actions grouped into meaningful parts, and nonverbal behavior also includes the whole encyclopedic underlying event sequence or network of the society. Each of the three types of behavior can be found in relation to smaller units related in sequences to make up larger ones, or as in a network of larger patterns of patterns.

[a] Sounds enter syllables, which enter rhythm groups, which enter even larger phonological sequences—and into matrices of sound types at various levels of size. Nonverbal behavior has significant chunks which are components of larger sequences which themselves are not necessarily parts of planned or intended meanings. For example, we have already shown how differences in specific sounds, across languages, can cause cultural misunderstanding—as in the word "pig" discussed in 2a above.

More general differences can also give problems. For example, if one is perceived as speaking too loudly, it is rude in some cultures. Within American culture to do so within certain contexts, e.g., within a library or hospital, is culturally inappropriate. To do so in some cultures can be seen as unfriendly, or as being too pushy.

Staring at a person can be variously interpreted across cultures. In a French cultural setting, for example, if a young woman makes eye contact with a young man at a bus station, it indicates that she may want to have an affair or alternatively it may result in sexual harassment. Similarly, Kathie Dooley (personal communication) reports that for the foreign woman in Brazil to look a man in the face was interpreted as a "come-on". When getting on a bus, or when meeting a stranger, she found she had to be careful where she looked. While she as an American was seeking to try to show herself to be friendly by smiling and looking people in the eye, to Brazilians this had a different implication. Similarly, a friendly American "goodbye" wave might be interpreted by some Brazilians as "come here".

In the Bajju culture, in a situation where a parent is disciplining a child, that child should not make eye contact with that parent. If that child continues to look or stare at the parent, that action connotes defiance on the part of the child. Contrastively, an American parent when disciplining a child may require his child to look at him in order to indicate that he or she is really listening.

Staring in some situations may be merely curiosity at the sight of skin or hair color of a foreigner. Ward (1984:117) says that in some cases (in order to avoid being bothered by the stare) one must look away and "forget it". In a Singapore subway, Hugoniot tells Pike, all passengers—both men and women—avoid eye contact.

Spatial distance may be an analog of voice quality. C. McKinney (1993: 57) points out that being too close to a Choctaw speaker damaged the research the student was undertaking. As the student moved closer to the Choctaw speaker, he found he had more and more trouble hearing what the speaker said. By so doing he was violating that speaker's space. By backing off he suddenly found that he could again hear what was said, a result that ran contrary to his expectations.

In a classroom K. Pike on occasion has asked students to move to the distance they would find appropriate for talking to a close friend. The distance they chose was quite close. Similarly, when asked to move to a distance they were comfortable with in relating in a classroom with their professor, they moved about ten feet away!

In some cultures, we feel uncomfortable when speakers come so close to us that they seem to be "breathing down our necks". In some instances, taking hold of a person's elbow is considered to be friendly; in others it would be misunderstood as a nuisance. In a Bajju cultural context a buyer will grab the elbow of a seller in a market context in order to attract that seller's attention. In fact, the day the McKinneys sold out their household goods was the day they discovered this cultural practice. Carol found her elbows ached by the end of the day! Morain (1978:11) points out, that for some Americans, relaxing may include putting one's feet up on the furniture —but this action shocked a Colombian hostess who perceived it as disgusting.

Gestures often have significance in one culture different from their meanings in another culture. For example, in an American cultural context shaking one's fist at another individual indicates aggression. In northern Nigeria shaking one's fist at another individual indicates honor, and this gesture is accompanied by the phrase "May you have long life!"

Storti (1989:22) quotes Hall about a further physical component: "to the Arab smells are pleasing . . . to smell one's friend is not only nice but desirable . . . whereas Americans, . . . trained as they are not to breathe in people's faces, automatically communicate shame in trying to be polite."

K. Pike has seen a British phonetician identify the dialect of a speaker who just walked into a classroom, by the way he walked! Dialect of speech and dialect of physical walking behavior were tied into the same cultural background!

[b] Sounds enter into standard sequences in a language, to make up words which in turn enter sequences of words with intended meanings in expected contexts. So, also, body posture or gestures or deliberate actions

can enter into sequences which are deliberately meaningful, or intended, in a larger context.

For example, words like "pig" are made up of sounds, but then as a whole enter into larger wholes such as "The little pig went to market". The way this differs from "I saw the little pig" is part of grammar. (For methodology of the analysis, and extensive illustrations, including relation to a story as a whole, see Kenneth L. Pike and Evelyn G. Pike 1982, 2nd ed.)

Physical intended combinations of gestures or actions can also make up meaningful wholes. In baseball, the attempt to hit the ball into the outfield differs emically from an attempt for a bunt. Such actions are comparable to words in language. The combination of a batter trying to bunt so as to allow a person from third base to run to home plate is like a sentence combining words—it is more than a gesture by itself, and it carries a larger meaning like a tiny story, or a chapter of a story.

[c] The social and personal background to a story, and the actual order or interlocking of its happenings, is the referential structure (using tagmemic terms—other theories handle the material differently, listing phonology, grammar, and semantics as a trio, rather than the tagmemic trio of phonology, grammar, and reference, each with its semantic impact in different ways). In language, the way of telling a story is grammatical—with the teller presenting different parts of an event in any order chosen by him; what the telling is about (is being referred to) is referential. Its sequence is chronological and thus is invariant. (If the telling follows the order of the happening, then the two sequences are for that moment isomorphic, but it need not remain that way in other tellings.)

The referential structure includes the networks (matrices) of social relations of kin, and country, and race. Belonging to a society is necessary to avoid loneliness. Lack of communication on a friendly basis with others can lead to devastating damage. Language and other social interaction are a part of the necessary background, along with courtesy and trust, if one wishes to avoid cross-cultural misunderstanding and loss of friendship. Desperate loneliness, it seems to us, might be labeled, metaphorically, as a kind of "hell on earth". In order to avoid it, one seeks for ways for companionship, reconciliation, justice, and relation to a religion which helps bind folk together—if one is a theist—to nonhuman realities. Personal hurt, of many kinds, is sad. Social cohesion is one way to lessen such hurts.

In this sense, we put person above logic, with higher priority than things or argumentation. Tagmemics searches for a linguistics, an anthropology, and a philosophy which is in this sense holistic and useful beyond mere language.

[d] Poetry is one way in which the three hierarchies integrate in producing desired intents. (Again, a holistic view is needed for this practical

understanding of communication.)

In poetry if one makes two words to rhyme, the reader may be forced to join them mentally (consciously or unconsciously) in ways he might not otherwise have expected. At the same time, the meaning of the words which rhyme is tied into referential background meanings, and the larger (holistic) included meaning forced into attention. In addition, items may be repeated again and again, with that very repetition also having a semantic (explicit or implicit) impact, but carried by the repetitive lexical-grammatical structure.

The following poem (by Pike 1986:16), however, is quite different. It uses two stresses per line (which is one kind of rhythm group), with the last two written lines comprising a single group. In addition, there is a semantic (referential) tie where "alone" relates to the words "apart", "isolation", and the phrases "would die" and "kills me".

ALONE, KILLS ME
I cannot live
Apart from others—
Self would die
If goal achieved
Is isolation.
Let me be myself,
With you ...
TALK to me!

4. *Four Universal Underlying Characteristics (Comparable to Four Cells in a Tagmemic Unit) Interlock, but with Clashing Manifestations in Different Cultures*

[a] The tagmemic theory, developed initially to deal with linguistic data, is a holistic one (Pike 1967 [1954]). It treats human action as a totality in relation to its world environment, and it is a totality which cannot be split into autonomous parts (Pike 1985). For example, it has insisted that phonological analysis needs grammatical prerequisites (Pike 1947, 1956). The parts of life and living can be partially separated, so that they can have studies concentrated on those parts. The difficulty comes when one tries to assume that these parts are in fact totally separate without inescapable ties to, or reliance on, other parts.

[b] The theory deals with a tagmeme which includes four components:

The first component is the *set* (or list, or one selection from the list) of items, actions, thoughts, etc.—the *substance*—which may come within some one position; this set is technically called a *class*. Noun phrases, for example, are often part of a set of items which can occur in the subject position.

The second component is the *position* (in time, or space, or sequence of action, or of a point in a matrix) with the technical term of *slot*. The position of subject of a sentence is a grammatical slot. The position of a vowel in a syllable is a phonological one. The position of a father in a kinship system is a referential one.

The third component of a tagmeme is the *function*—or purpose, or cause—of the item in the position mentioned; and technically it is called a *role*. The subject of a clause may be an actor (or in a passive clause it may be the recipient or undergoer of the action).

The fourth component is the *governance* (technically, its *cohesion*). It is the background system locally affecting or controlling the events or items as they occur in a position with a certain role. In phonology such a cohesion system might be the riming pattern, in part; in grammar, an insistence on agreement of subject with predicate; in referential structure, the unconscious personal cognitive structure or physical constraints of members of the cast. (Some scholars might prefer to call the cohesion system a "frame of reference", or [phenomenologically] the "horizon".)

Poetry, which we discussed very briefly in the last section, can integrate all of these items into a single coherent larger system. In any integration all four components must be present.

If one changes the focus of discussion so that, for example, a certain "purpose" comes under attention as if it were a "thing" in the class (substance) cell, then something else will move to fill in the expected blank. In this, the tagmemic system reflects structure like a kaleidoscope—the parts (analogous to bits of glass) remain the same in the equipment, but the bits under attention vary, and change the pattern impact. (For an illustration of this—which is too large to replicate here—see Pike 1988, where a simple poem is told seven different ways, retaining the same background cognitive content or relationships, but with a different grammatical focus.)

[c] Each tagmemic unit—or part of a unit—may have sharply different ways of integrating the four behavioral/cognitive components to each other, and to other cultures. This leads potentially to very difficult cross-cultural problems of adjustment for persons coming into another culture. (Our illustrations will be mostly of Americans going elsewhere—because of our birth biases—but the theory and methodology should work equally well in other directions.)

For example, one of my (Pike) biggest blunders was in Asia. I had previously spent several years in Latin America, but I had never been involved with Muslim people. Now, however, I was in a meeting with a very high government official of one of the Asian countries. After lengthy discussion of technical matters the official asked me a question something like,

"Why do you enjoy linguistics?" I replied, "It's delightful, like eating a ham sandwich!" OUCH! Muslims do not eat such meat! In relation to the tagmemic substance or class of the interchange, I had not thought of its place in the contrastive cohesion/governance structures of our respective religious beliefs, where his rejected ham but mine did not. In terms of the role/function component, my purpose was to illustrate my answer with an intelligible metaphor—but it potentially clashed mentally with his underlying purpose of following his religious practices.

In a second class/substance illustration, Asians would prefer that one person pay the bill rather than dividing it up, when (slot/position) they go out to lunch together. This social judgment (cohesion/governance) avoids potential embarrassment (role/function).

In another example where potential cross-cultural misunderstanding may occur, Asians, at a meal (slot/place), leave a bit on their plates (class/ substance)—versus Americans (differing by cohesion/governance) who "clean their plates". In the former case, the Asians signal that they do not wish more (role/function)—but Americans in Asia may get more than they wish. Similarly Africans may signal that they do not want further to drink by turning their glasses or cups upside-down. If they are left right-side up, the hostess assumes that her guests want more to drink.

Again taking an Asian example: in playing tennis (class/substance), it is best to try to be friendly and to have a good time (role/function), not to put emphasis on winning—this shows politeness to a guest (cohesion/governance) when entertaining him (slot/position). Here the maintenance of good interpersonal relationships outranks any emphasis on competition and winning.

In another example, one that applies widely in non-American cultural contexts, being on time (slot/position) and getting to the point (class/ substance) is a value (role/function) for westerners (cohesion/governance); but making a guest feel comfortable (class/substance) is an Asian value (role/function). Similarly developing good interpersonal relations precedes time or business in many societies. An American time orientation tends to interfere with developing good interpersonal relations, relationships that take time to develop. Americans tend to state their business first, then work on developing good interpersonal relations. In many cultures the converse it true. To work effectively in such cultural contexts Americans need to change their modes of relating. Business does not come first; people do!

In China (Seligman 1989:29) when introduced to strangers (slot/ position), Chinese sometimes do not smile (class/substance). Their society leads them (cohesion/governance) to keep feelings hidden rather than to express them (role/function)—although by so doing they are not representing anger, or negative feelings.

A second Chinese example relates to greetings after a long absence. Though an American typically might give a "bear-hug" to greet a friend following a long absence, a Chinese person would not do so. Both age and status are very important in Chinese culture, such that a bear-hug would not be acceptable between strangers, between men and women, or with older or higher ranked people. To be physically demonstrative is not acceptable (Seligman 1989:30).

In Irian Jaya Andrew Sims (personal communication) reports that two men who had flown from the highlands to the coast took their first automobile ride in a taxi. Their reaction was that they could not help wondering at how strong the people were who were pushing the trees and houses past the taxi so fast! In changing their environment (slot/place) from where there were no automobiles, their experience in the interior cultural environment conditioned their interpretation of new data (cohesion/governance). One must learn to live in a new environment, interpreting it in relation to a new understanding of some relations of cause and effect based on new data.

In some cultures there are areas of proprietary knowledge, knowledge that is not passed along to others or that is passed along only within certain restricted contexts (e.g., through lengthy apprenticeships). Sometimes this proprietary knowledge is retained because of an image of limited good (Foster 1965) where to share knowledge will mean that the person is losing some of his or her own knowledge. This use of knowledge differs radically from that of the west where we often speak of freedom of information. In the west the use of knowledge may be restricted in some specified contexts, e.g., through holding a patent. However, increasingly we are dealing with knowledge engineering where we seek to harness and make available widely useful information.

Areas in other cultures where knowledge tends to be treated as proprietary include religion, magic, herbalism, divination, and local medical systems. Other areas include various crafts (e.g., blacksmithing, tailoring, barbering, etc.). Eunice Pike ran into this use of proprietary knowledge when she taught a Mazatec woman how to make tatted lace. Eunice expected this woman to pass on this technique to others, many of whom had deep financial needs. She saw this new production technique as a potential source of income for Mazatec women. However, the Mazatec refused to do so, since they believed that abilities were like goods, limited (Foster 1965), and that a person who passed on such a new ability was in fact losing some of her own.

A common problem in cross-cultural situations is how to deal with petty theft. For example, Kathie Dooley (personal communication) reports that in Brazil a friend needed advice about how to complain about a neighbor walking off with her matches (class/substance). A chief advised her that if she asked about it directly, there would be a very hostile, angry response. Rather she should wait until the person was around who probably did it, and then innocently look around for the matches and say "I wonder what could have happened to the matches"—and the problem would get resolved peacefully. If the above situation is looked at tagmemically, the slot/position is the sharp difficulty unless the query were made in the appropriate place, with appropriate people present. Cohesion/governance involves habits of courtesy which are very powerful and involve interrogating people who might feel embarrassed. Finally, the role/function has a double aim: to stop the theft, and to avoid destroying a cultural friendship or the existing social environment.

More formal examples of cross-cultural misunderstanding occur when members of the dominant culture seek to relate to those of minority cultures, and specifically to apply the laws and customs of the dominant culture to people within the minority cultures. For example, Dave Farah (personal communication) reports that a Spanish judge set a certain time for a hearing on a land dispute between a Chipaya Indian group and Aymaras in Bolivia (class/substance). When the Chipaya Indians did not appear at the set time (slot/position), the judge ceded the land to the Aymaras. Since the Chipayas do not have the same way of viewing time, the exact time set by the Spanish judge did not seem relevant to them. What they wanted was justice in the court such that their land was defended. The Spanish expectation was that the legal system required the Chipayas to appear at the specific given time, as ordered by the Spanish judge. Too often minority groups lose land and rights through cross-cultural misunderstandings with dominant groups, as illustrated in this example.

Cross-cultural interpretation (cohesion/governance) involves not just words in relation to meanings as found in a dictionary—but in relation to cultural expectations. For example, there might be the courtesy of a "gentle" rejection that an outsider might not recognize. Factors such as intonation or idiomatic interpretations in relation to contexts also come into play. As Americans, we are likely to assume that words mean precisely what the dictionary seems to imply (role/function), and only with some difficulty do we grant a meaning that is clear to others but that is hidden to us. People in a culture use metaphor, special use of folktales or proverbs, or other means to accomplish such courteous purposes.

Similarly, metaphorical use of words may result in frustration when seeking to work cross-culturally. In some contexts when working with the Bajju, McKinney found that she understood every word said and still had not a clue as to what those words meant in that context. For example, when attending a Cherubim and Seraphim Church service, everyone started dancing to the back of the sanctuary. Her husband Norris indicated that she should too. When she asked why they were doing so he told her that the man next to him stated that they were "going to pour water!" Only when she got to the back of the sanctuary did she discover that "pouring water" in this context meant to give one's offering.

Clues to social status and cultural acceptability can often be found in the dialect of the language spoken by the individual. Cultural clashes can occur when social class and dialect spoken clash. For example, in Latin America Clarence Church (personal communication) reported on two American women who learned a variety of Spanish while living with Indians in their village. Later those women were invited as guests to a high status home in the capital city of that country. It was years before their hosts invited them back because their Spanish vocabulary had embarrassed their hosts. It was only when their speech became consistent with their bearing that they were invited back.

If looked at tagmemically, the slot/position of the women as of high status through being expatriates ran into problems by the way they spoke the national language. It lacked the elegance of people of a similar social status. And this language characteristic controlled, for their hosts, their evaluations of these two expatriates. In terms of role/function, various clues to social status and cultural acceptability can be found in the dialect one uses.

5. *Oral Societies*

Some cultures are basically oral societies, without a long history of having a written language. In terms of a particle, wave, and field approach to culture, orality would form the field for analysis of specific incidents (waves and particles) that take place. The suggestions below also apply where illiteracy is an issue or where literacy is a newly acquired skill. When an outsider from a society with a long literary tradition enters such a society, there are considerations that apply regardless of the formal educational level of those persons with whom he or she interacts.

In basically oral societies decisions need to be made orally without depending on some written format. For example, the outsider working with a basically oral society might want to write down alternatives to be considered in the decision process, as might occur within his or her own cultural background. However, use of a written form, such as writing down alternatives other than perhaps within the meeting itself, should be avoided. Decisions need to be made through oral discussion that leads to consensus. Consensual decision making of some form is the means whereby decisions tend to be made within basically oral societies. Each individual at the meeting has an opportunity to express his or her opinion, and thereby contribute to a democratically determined decision. A decision mechanism such as is outlined in *Roberts' Rules of Order* is foreign to many in basically oral societies. Voting, with the majority of votes cast deciding an issue, is also outside the usual means of decision making.

Another slot/position within which orality requires that an outsider interact in a culturally sensitive manner in order to avoid misunderstanding is the use of written communications. For example, once a decision is reached through a consensual decision making process, then that decision is written down. The McKinneys found that use of cc: on letters with multiple copies sent to different individuals did not elicit a response from anyone, even the person to whom the letter was addressed. The others copied assumed that the letter really was not for them, and the individual to whom the letter was addressed was offended by having copies of his letter sent to others. We found that each letter needed to be addressed to the individual to whom it was sent, and only to that individual.

In oral societies in order to avoid cross-cultural misunderstandings the outsider needs to conduct business on a face-to-face basis. If at all possible this includes avoiding use of the telephone, even when the phone is working. Body language, clarity of sound, and the potential for including more than two people are invaluable advantages in face-to-face communication.

From a western point of view, we expect that when we give out a form to be filled out, the recipient will understand the written directions and hopefully will be able to complete it correctly. It is always much safer when working in basically oral cultures to also communicate orally what information the form requires.

While the above considerations tend to apply when working with societies which are basically oral, many of those societies are experiencing rapid culture change. Some within them will depend more upon literacy skills and sources of information than others. As newspapers, primers, books, and other printed material are increasingly important worldwide, the individual working with a basically oral society can expect that some individuals will depend more on the printed word than others, though most even if literate still depend heavily upon oral communication. It is always safer to communicate your message orally than in written form for those from basically oral societies.

6. *Event Orientation versus Time Orientation*

Western cultures tend to be time orientated. Events occur on time, and if they do not, we tend to remark on it because it is inappropriate for them to occur late. If we state that an event is to occur at 11 a.m., it usually occurs at 11 a.m. For example, it would greatly embarrass a bride and her family for a wedding not to occur at the time stated on the wedding invitation. We commoditize time; we can waste time, spend time, save time, etc. We speak of work time versus leisure time. Here time is the field upon which events occur. Because of their time orientation, many westerners find this an area of great frustration and misunderstanding in cultures which have an entirely different approach to time.

Many other cultures are event or personal relationship orientated. What is important is that everything is ready and all the interpersonal relationships are in place before an event can occur. This means that one's whole approach to time orientation needs to shift or that individual may face stress induced disorders such as stomach ulcers and stress related headaches.

McKinney remembers one wedding that began four hours after the time stated on the printed wedding invitation. In order not to arrive hours before the wedding actually occurred, she simply stayed home until she saw the vehicles with the bridal party pass her home; then she went to the wedding.

Though local protocol differs, typically the event begins once the guest of honor arrives. Since in many instances it is impolite to arrive after the guest of honor does, the honored guest knows that he or she needs to arrive at least an hour late in order to allow others time to come.

Because many are increasingly aware of a difference between time orientation and event orientation, some now state on what type of time an event is to occur. By so doing people are seeking to ameliorate the problems of causing people to wait hours. A posted notice of a meeting of a union for junior staff at a Nigerian university urged "Not African time please!"

Johnson (1994 [1978]) compared the French approach to time with that of the Machiguenga in the Amazon rain forest in Peru. For purposes of comparison he divided time into three categories: production time, consumption time, and free time. He found that the French exceeded the Machiguenga in work time both within and outside the home. The French similarly exceeded the Machiguenga in consumption time. And the Machiguengas far exceeded the French in free time. Johnson stated his reaction to this difference in use of time, "It happens each time I return to their communities that, after a period of two or three days, I sense a definite decrease in time pressure; this is a physiological as well as a psychological sensation" (1994:137). The sense of hurry is gone as is the time pressure of our time famine western society. So while there are adjustments to be made when moving from a time orientated society to an event or interpersonal relationship oriented one, there are also refreshing rewards to be gained.

7.   An Emic View of Truth

At one meeting McKinney attended, as the discussion proceeded, one person stated emphatically, "I'm interested in truth, not culture!" While we do not want to tackle the sticky question of what is truth here, perhaps it is sufficient to state that truth is mediated through culture. There are different fields of truth in different cultures.

In another culture one needs to learn how truth is articulated. For example, in some cultures it is impolite to answer any question with a "No". So if asked a question to which the logical answer is "no", how will an individual respond where he or she is culturally constrained from saying "no"? Typically, he or she will tell you what s/he expects you will want to hear, even when meaning "no". When you as the outsider finally get the message, as by the individual not showing up when you invited him or her to a meal, you will typically feel frustrated and lied to.

Part of working effectively cross-culturally involves understanding means by which negation can be expressed. Typically, you can save yourself a lot of frustration by learning how to ask questions in a culturally appropriate way. For example, you might ask, "Would Monday at 10 a.m. be good for a meeting, or would some other time be better?" That way people have the alternative of stating another time rather than simply answering "yes" when in fact they mean "no".

In a culture that stresses good interpersonal relationships, maintaining those relationships may be more important than truth. Those relationships are also more important than any business that you may want to conduct. In Russia male business executives tend to get to know each other in steam baths. After the interpersonal relationships are developed, then you can conduct your business.

Where interpersonal relations are central, expect that people will tell you what they think you want to hear. For Americans, who expect straightforward responses, there will be adjustments in order to learn to work with an entirely different orientation.

8. *Ethnicity*

By ethnicity we are speaking of the field that involves a sense of common identity that a group of people have. The most salient feature of that common identity is language. In addition, they have common customs, history, origins narrative, a sense of "we-ness", and common traditions. Many modern nation states today are really nations of nations. People's primary identity is with reference to their own ethnic nation state, not to the modern nation state that is recognized by their having a representative in the United Nations.

In an African context people's primary allegiance is to their ethnic group, their tribe. Only secondarily is it to the nation in which they reside. All those who belong to the same ethnic group are one's brothers and sisters. This kinship model of relating helps to maintain that sense of unity.

Ethnicity has its advantages as well as its problems. For example, to work with one's ethnic brothers and sisters gives security. Lamb writes about this identity as follows:

> One day in Uganda I was talking with a U.S. diplomat at the embassy. His secretary entered the office and said a man was waiting to see him. "Is he Ugandan?" the diplomat asked. "No, he's Acholi," she answered. Her implication was clear: in Uganda, there were Acholis and other tribalists, but no Ugandans. One's identity was tribal, not national (Lamb 1985:11).

When working in a country with multiple ethnic groups, expect that conflict will occur along ethnic lines. Further, expect that voting in national elections will reflect the ethnic divisions of that country. And expect that crime will occur more readily across ethnic lines than within an ethnic group.

While modern nation states work at developing a sense of allegiance to the state, underlying that allegiance is often ethnicity. It is better to enjoy and appreciate that diversity that each ethnic group can bring to the modern nation state than to seek to squelch it. For example, some ethnic groups are inclined to commerce, others to modern technology, others to farming, others to handcrafts, etc.

A common means of seeking to squelch ethnicity is through imposing a dominant language upon a minority people. This language dominance may result in cultural death to the minority language or the relegation of the minority language primarily to oral contexts.

9.   Obtaining Useful Emic Advice

In order to avoid cross-cultural misunderstandings and cultural clashes to the extent possible, it is important to obtain useful emic advice for working effectively within a second language and culture context. Certainly learning the local language is a good starting point, as many of the basic assumptions about reality of that second culture are encoded within their language. Secondly, read widely on the second language and culture. Search out what other researchers have written, and check out the extent to which their findings apply in your situation. And thirdly, by all means seek the emic advice and knowledge of local people. They understand their culture, and are often more than willing to share it with a responsive outsider.

10. Culture as Particle, Wave, and Field

Since cultures are interrelated wholes or fields, when entering a new culture we tend to see only the particles of that new culture. We tend not to see and understand the interrelated aspects of that new culture, the waves if you will.

This particle view of culture can result in incredible culture shock and stress to the outsider. "Culture shock is the psychological anxiety and consequences that people experience when entering and working within another culture" (McKinney 1993:32). It occurs when people lose their familiar cues to normal social interaction. Those cues include gestures, language, customs and norms, common presuppositions, and knowledge of how to interact in a normally acceptable manner.

When an individual first encounters a cross-cultural situation, he or she may feel a euphoria at the newness and excitement of that which is different. We might compare that euphoria to getting one's feet wet within a wave. However, after an initial honeymoon stage when living cross-culturally, things begin to grate on you. In terms of a wave analogy, you might well feel like you are drowning. There are too many changes in social interaction and you feel overwhelmed. This stage typically occurs before that of good cross-cultural adjustment.

There are several typical reactions to the drowning stage. For example, you might want to flee the situation, or you might over-identify with the new cultural context, perhaps by rejecting your own cultural context, or you might find yourself overly critical of the new situation. Other alternatives include becoming depressed, idolizing your home culture, retreating into an expatriate ghetto of one's own culture, and in general minimizing contact with those within the new culture. Over time gradually the particles of the new situation begin to make sense. Cross-cultural misunderstanding lessens. This is particularly true if the individual takes the time to learn the language of the people within the second culture.

Areas that are especially stressful in a second language context include lying, cheating, theft, envy, jealousy, poverty, suspicion, meanness, unpaid loans, bribery, corruption, and on occasion even violence. It helps to remember that most of us have trouble with these same issues within our own comfortable culture, and they upset us in our own culture as well.

11. *Emic Cross-Cultural Understandings and Misunderstandings in Perspective*

In this paper we have explored various areas of emic cross-cultural understandings and misunderstandings. We have done so first by looking at them from the perspective of fields composed of waves and particles, a phenomenon that we also identified in language.

We began by pointing to the importance of names and categorization in cross-cultural perspective. By naming something, by word or phrase, we can refer to it, explain it, and recognize it. Names of animals, minerals, vegetables, and other phenomena fit together into categories, categories that it is often useful to view as components in taxonomies. The bases of those taxnomies tend to be culture or culture area specific.

We next discussed the fact that native speakers react to emic units of culture, in spite of the fact that there are etic differences. For example, a car is a car whether it is a Mercedes Benz or a Toyota.

In terms of emic units within languages, we noted that one's language places constraints upon one's abilities to speak another language. We discussed the difficulty of the Mixtec speaker pronouncing the English word "pig"; he experienced the constraints placed upon him by the phonological structure of Mixtec.

We briefly explored some culture universals, such as eating, sleeping, having families, and dealing with anger and aggression, though noting that these have significant local variants. To work effectively cross-culturally, it is important to understand those local variants. We noted that both form and meaning are required for human emic units and systems.

Entities occur in part-whole hierarchies of three types, each of which extends tagmemic linguistic theory to cultural data. We discussed some examples of potential cross-cultural misunderstandings, as, for example, with respect to space, voice quality, gestures, and eye contact or lack thereof. Tagmemic linguistic theory is holistic and as such it views language and culture from a holistic perspective.

We also noted the metaphorical nature of both language and culture. Lack of understanding of relevant metaphor can lead to cross-cultural misunderstandings.

In the latter sections of this paper we explored some fields that hopefully will help an outsider understand a second cultural context. So we explored the implications of working with oral societies or with new literates, time orientation versus event or interpersonal relationship orientation, truth as mediated through culture, and ethnicity. The beginning step to avoiding cross-cultural misunderstandings must be learning the language of that culture, and language and cultural learning are a dyad that cannot be separated.

REFERENCES

Barfield, Owen. 1967. *Speaker's Meaning.* Middletown, CT: Wesleyan University Press.

Bruner, Jerome S. 1974 [1972]. *The Relevance of Education.* Harmonsworth, Middlesex: Penguin Books.

Denny, J. Peter & Chet A. Creider. 1986. "The Semantics of Noun Classes in Proto Bantu." *Noun Classes and Categorization: Proceedings of a*

Symposium on Categorization and Noun Classification. Edited by Colette Craig, 217-239. Amsterdam & Philadelphia: John Benjamins.

Foster, George M. 1965. "Peasant Society and the Image of Limited Good." *American Anthropologist* 67.293-315.

Gadamer, Hans-Georg. 1976 [1966]. *Philosophical Hermeneutics.* Translated and edited by David E. Linge. Berkeley, CA: Univ. of California Press.

Geertz, Clifford 1973. *The Interpretation of Cultures.* New York, NY: Basic Books, Inc.

Goodenough, Ward Hunt. 1981 [1971]. *Culture, Language, and Society.* 2nd ed. Menlo Park, CA: Benjamin-Cummings Publishing Co.

Headland, Thomas N., Kenneth L. Pike & Marvin Harris, eds. 1990. *Emics and Etics: The Insider/Outsider Debate.* Newbury Park, CA: Sage Publications.

Johnson, Alan. 1994 [1978]. "In Search of the Affluent Society." *Applying Cultural Anthropology: An Introductory Reader.* 2nd ed. Edited by Aaron Podolefsky & Peter J. Brown, 133-140. Mountain View, CA: Mayfield Publishing Co.

Kant, Immanuel. 1966 [1785]. *The Fundamental Principles of the Metaphysic of Ethics.* Translated by Otto Manthey-Zorn [1938]. New York, NY: Appleton-Century-Crofts.

Kay, Paul. 1971. "Taxonomy and Semantic Contrast." *Language* 47.866-887.

Kondo, Riena. 1991. "Taking into Consideration Cultural Learning Styles." *Notes on Literacy* 17:2.23-34.

Lakoff, George. 1987. *Women, Fire and Dangerous Things: What Categories Reveal about the Mind.* Chicago, IL: University of Chicago Press.

Lamb, David. 1985. *The Africans.* Rev. ed. New York, NY: Vintage Books.

McKinney, Carol V. 1993. *Globe Trotting in Sandals: A Field Guide to Cultural Research.* 2nd preliminary ed. Dallas, TX: McKinney.

Morain, Genelle G. 1978. *Kinesics and Cross-Cultural Understanding.* Arlington, VA: Center for Applied Linguistics.

Patrick, George Thomas W. 1889 [1888]. *The Fragments of the Work of Heraclitus of Ephesus on Nature* [transl. from the Greek text of Bywater]. Baltimore, MD: N. Murray.

Pike, Evelyn G. & Rachel Saint, eds. 1988. *Workpapers Concerning Waorani Discourse Features.* Dallas, TX: Summer Institute of Linguistics.

Pike, Kenneth L. 1947. "Grammatical Prerequisites to Phonemic Analysis." Word 3.155-171.

——————. 1956. "More on Grammatical Prerequisites." *Word* 8.106-121.

——————. 1959. "Language as Particle, Wave and Field." *The Texas Quarterly* 2.37-54.

——————. 1967 [1954, 1955, 1960]. *Language in Relation to a Unified Theory of the Structure of Human Behavior*. The Hague: Mouton.

——————. 1985. "The Need for Rejection of Autonomy in Linguistics." *The Eleventh LACUS Forum 1984*, pp. 35-54. Edited by Robert A. Hall, Jr. Columbia, SC: Hornbeam Press.

——————. 1986. "On the Value of Local Languages." *Languages in the International Perspective (Delaware Symposium 3)*, pp. 13-19. Edited by Nancy Schweda-Nicholson. Norwood, NJ: Ablex.

——————. 1988 [1975]. "Bridging Language Learning, Language Analysis, and Poetry, via Experimental Syntax." *Linguistics in Context: Connecting Observation and Understanding*. Edited by Deborah Tannen. Norwood, NJ: Ablex.

Pike, Kenneth L. & Evelyn G. Pike. 1982. *Grammatical Analysis*. 2nd ed. Dallas, TX: Summer Institute of Linguistics and the University of Texas at Arlington.

Polanyi, Michael. 1969. *Knowing and Being: Essays*. Edited by Marjorie Grene. Chicago, IL: University of Chicago Press.

Polanyi, Michael & Harry Prosch. 1975. *Meaning*. Chicago, IL: University of Chicago Press.

Searle, John. 1984. *Minds, Brains, and Science*. Cambridge: Harvard University Press.

Seligman, Scott D. 1989. *Dealing with the Chinese: A Practical Guide to Business Etiquette in the People's Republic Today*. New York, NY: Warren Books.

Storti, Craig. 1989. *The Art of Crossing Cultures*. Yarmouth, ME: Intercultural Press.

Ward, Ted Warren. 1984. *Living Overseas: A Book of Preparations*. New York, NY: Free Press.

THE IMPORTANCE OF PURPOSIVE
BEHAVIOR IN TEXT ANALYSIS

KENNETH L. PIKE AND DONALD A. BURQUEST
Summer Institute of Linguistics
University of Texas at Arlington

1. *Introduction*

The foundational assumption underlying this paper is that human behavior is purposive. We will demonstrate in two different ways that this notion of purpose influences the behavior of individuals in specific ways in
their own situations. First, we will show how an author's purpose influences
the form a given text takes; secondly, we will show how the purposes and
character of participants in the text (provided that they are well drawn and
representative of human beings who might in fact exist in the real world)
influence their behavior as well. In our demonstration we will argue that
text analysis—discourse grammar—requires more than the simple analysis
of the text itself; specifically, events which are not even presented in a text
may play a major role in its analysis. As an aid to the reader, we have
elected to present our findings in a relatively brief and summary manner,
attempting to avoid technical jargon; for those who may be interested in
further details, we include in the appendices a more extensive collection of
the facts upon which we base our analysis.

A non-fictional narrative is an account of reality, but of course it is not
the reality itself. In particular, such a narrative account omits reference to
many events that in fact took place, and those which are presented may be
presented in a sequential ordering which does not match the chronological
ordering in which they took place in the real world being reported on. Nor
is this a characteristic only of non-fictional works; it is a common trait of
effective fiction that it must have the markings of a non-fictional presentation, in fact matching possible reality at least to the extent that it draws
the reader into a state of "suspension of disbelief."

These constraints on presentation within a narrative are not accidental.
The fact that not all events are reported in such accounts is partly a function
of the fact that some events are not relevant to the account. For example,
they may be below the threshold of attention (to walk down the street involves a sequence of muscle movements which are commonly not mentioned); or they may simply be events which are not in focus (the sun
comes up every day, though it often is not mentioned as doing so); or the
events may be entailed by the presentation of other events which are part
of the same script and thus predictable (to drive down the street involves
getting into a car, sitting down, starting the engine, etc.). Of course, if there
is some fact particularly of interest in such cases, details not normally mentioned may instead become the very focus of attention (muscle soreness because of a particularly strenuous encounter with evil the night before may
make the walk down the street one in which details of muscle movement
are particularly important).

By contrast, in other cases an event may not be reported in a narrative
for rhetorical reasons, perhaps simply because the narrator wishes to height-

en tension. For example, in the accounts to be reported on here, all from the 'detective' genre, the narrator knows the identity of the person committing the crime and the details surrounding the crime, but to recount the event at the outset would dramatically reduce the tension in the story and thus reader interest.[1]

Consider in addition the fact that even those events which are recounted do not always match in order the sequencing of actual occurrence. Partly this is a simple consequence of the fact that several events can take place simultaneously in the real world, but they cannot be reported on simultaneously because a linguistic message by its nature is necessarily sequenced. We propose that even in those instances in which the simultaneous events are reported as quickly as possible within the same sequence, however, the actual sequencing chosen by the narrator is important and reflects intent and purpose. Further, there are also instances in which the narrator chooses deliberately to portray events in an order different from that in which they actually occurred, again for rhetorical effectiveness (we return to this topic below).

During his career, Rex Stout published a total of forty-six detective novels featuring private investigator Nero Wolfe as main character. In this paper we investigate five of these: *Invitation to Murder*, *The Zero Clue*, and *This Won't Kill You* are characterized by the publisher as "short novels" and published together in the book *Three Men Out*; the first in the series was *Fer-de-Lance*, which we consider as representative of Stout's initial technique; we include *Too Many Women* as an additional work to round out the sample.[2] We focus here mainly on *The Zero Clue*, making reference to the

---

[1] It is a matter of some interest that authors use different strategies in this regard. The works we will be reporting on by Rex Stout follow the pattern of delaying recounting the crime as summarized above, while works within the same detective genre having to do with the Columbo character typically present the details of the crime relatively early in the narrative and have as the story the steps Columbo follows to identify the criminal and bring him or her to justice.

[2] These works have all been reprinted, some several times. The following are the initial publication date (in parentheses with the title), and the date of the paperback version consulted for this research (in parentheses with the publisher of note): *Fer-de-Lance* (1934), Pyramid Books (NY: Pyramid Communications, 1964). *Three Men Out* (1952), Bantam Books (NY: Bantam Doubleday Dell, 1954). *Too Many Women* (1947), Bantam Books (NY: The Viking Press, 1975). Page numbers in the text and appendices refer to the texts as presented in the paperback editions. As an aid to determining the point in each narrative where the information being referred to is found, the following may be helpful: the text of *Fer-de-Lance* is 191 pages; that of *Too Many Women* is 168 pages; in *Three Men Out*, *Invitation to Murder* occupies pages 1-52, *The Zero*

other works only infrequently as further illustration of our discussion.

The crux of our proposal is that text analysis cannot be limited to an analysis of the linguistic structure of the text itself. Rather, as alluded to above, it is important also to consider the narrator's purpose, in particular as manifested in terms of the choice of which events to portray and in what order, and in addition, the personal characteristics of the participants in the text and the effect of those characteristics on their actions and thus the interpretation of those actions. Both of these matters lie outside the text itself in a real sense (indeed, some of the relevant personal characteristics of participants can be derived only from works distinct from those directly under study) and thus crucially are not part of the discourse (grammatical) structure. We will refer to such matters as the **referential structure** which the text relates to.[3]

2.   *Summary of The Zero Clue*

A brief summary of The Zero Clue is as follows. A probability expert (Leo Heller) is found murdered, apparently by one of his clients. While the approximate time of his death can be determined, there are six individuals who can reasonably be suspected. There is but one clue as to the identity of the murderer, a cryptic arrangement of pencils on Heller's desk (apparently left deliberately by Heller). Nero Wolfe, the main character of the story (*Nero* may be a pun on the word *hero*), conducts interviews with each suspect individually, in the presence of the police (including the recurrent character Inspector Cramer) and his own assistant (Archie Goodwin, consistently the viewpoint character of all the narratives of the series), then meets with the group as a whole. In the combined meeting, Wolfe relates Heller's clue to an explosion at a hospital some time before (the clue represents the number 302, the total number of people killed in the explosion), and he is able to flush a confession from one of the suspects (Jack Ennis, an inventor) by threatening to investigate which of them had been at the hospital at the time of the disaster.

3.   *Ordering of Events in The Zero Clue*

There are striking differences between the order in which crucial events are presented in the text, and the order in which they actually (that is to say, referentially) took place. To a very large extent, the telling of the story

---

Clue pages 53-103, *This Won't Kill You* pages 104-150.

[3] For full discussion of referential structure as constituting the referential hierarchy of tagmemics, see Kenneth L. Pike and Evelyn G. Pike, *Text and Tagmeme*. Norwood, NJ: Ablex, 1983.

follows the chronological happening, so it is those events in which this is not the case which demand our attention. We are particularly interested in considering the rhetorical purposes of Stout in this skewing between the referential sequencing and the text sequencing. The events of the story are presented in their order of narration (with the exception of a flashback to be discussed below) in Appendix B, which may be consulted for a fuller account.

We note first of all that the story opens with Goodwin visiting Heller's office. He will be unable to find him (his body is later discovered by the police), and it will turn out that all six of the suspects are on the scene already and will be introduced to the reader (though not all by name at this time). The first example of skewing we find is that upon Goodwin's entering the building in which Heller's office is located, there is a narration of a flashback by Goodwin in which he relates events of the preceding day; in particular, he is rebuked by Wolfe for interrupting him while he was tending to his orchids (a favorite hobby of his, based upon its recurrence in other works involving him), and especially so because his interruption is to inquire as to whether Wolfe is interested in helping Heller with an investigative problem which Heller has contacted Wolfe's office regarding. A summary of earlier negative experience between Wolfe and Heller is presented as explanation for why Wolfe is not interested in helping Heller and thus why Goodwin (always on the lookout for possible employment opportunities for his boss) must proceed alone at this point.

This skewing between the ordering of events textually as opposed to referentially is shown in the text itself by the form of comments made by Goodwin as viewpoint character. After the opening narrative positions him having encountered a woman in the lobby of Heller's building, the following sentences are found (p. 54):

> I'll have to let her stand there a minute while I explain that I was actually not on an operation at all. Chiefly, I was satisfying my own curiosity. At five in the afternoon the day before, in Nero Wolfe's office, there had been a phone call. After taking it I had gone to the kitchen ... to get a glass of water, and told Fritz [the chef] I was going upstairs [to the plant room] ...
> ... Fritz protested, but there was a gleam in his eye ...
> I went up three flights ...

The call, of course, was Heller's. Note the use of the temporal expression *in the afternoon the day before*, which places the event temporally prior in relation to the "present" of the narrative itself, and the use of the past perfect *there had been a phone call*. Such linguistic devices are often used to show the relative sequencing of events. It is interesting in this instance, however, that following two (or at most, three) occurrences of the past perfect tense, the account returns to simple past (... *Fritz protested* .... *I went up three flights* ....), though still within the flashback. The flashback itself contains a second flashback, an explanation of why Wolfe did not wish to be involved with Heller. Note the following (p. 55):

> Leo Heller had been tagged by fame. ... While making a living as a professor of mathematics ... he had begun, for amusement, to apply the laws of probability ... to various current events. Checking back on his records after a couple of years, he had been startled and pleased to find that the answers he had got from his formulas had been 86.3 per cent correct, and he had written a piece about it for a magazine.

This embedded flashback, continuing for several more sentences, is (with one exception, late in the text) all in past perfect tense. The return to the larger flashback is manifested by the following sentence (pp. 55-56):

> That had been three years ago, and now he was sitting pretty.

There seems to be some evidence, then, that use of the past perfect tense tends to identify events which are important to the account, but which are out of sequence. The difference in usage between flashbacks which consistently use past perfect (the second example above) and those which use past perfect only to introduce the flashback (the first example above) remains to be investigated and will not be discussed further here.

Now, what is Stout's purpose in relating these particular events in a flashback and not in chronological order within the text itself? Here we suggest that one of Stout's purposes in writing is to establish a problem, for which the remainder of the text will provide a solution. To grasp the reader's attention, there must be a "hook" in the early paragraphs, or the reader is likely to select another text to read; should the reader not be arrested by the beginning portion of the text and thus turn elsewhere, Stout will have failed to achieve what we consider his primary purpose, that of communicating (and of course, selling books and thereby making a living).

The second example of skewing of the ordering of events involves earlier relevant activities of all participants up to the time when Goodwin arrives at Heller's building. This includes information highly important to the story, including especially the following two types:

> Heller's background and the growth of his reputation as a prob-

ability expert (this is already discussed above in relation to Goodwin's narrative flashback).

The motivations of the six suspects for visiting Heller (which will not come out until they are interviewed much later by Wolfe).

Recall that this work is in the 'detective' genre. While a different strategy is possible (see mention of narratives involving the Columbo character in footnote 1), it is not uncommon in detective works for the reader to be invited along on the mystery. Indeed, the puzzle aspect of such narratives may be a primary reason for their popularity. It is as if the author and reader are involved in a game, perhaps a competition—the author challenges the reader to identify the person who committed the crime before the detective in the story does so. To invite the reader's participation in this genre, however, requires that there be some mystery to be solved. It is not unlike an account within the 'adventure' genre, in which the hero is embroiled in some state of affairs which seems to offer no means for escape; unless the character is more clever than the reader (so that the reader cannot find the solution the character ultimately comes to), the story lacks impact. In this particular story, Heller's background, and the events leading up to the tension between him and Wolfe and Goodwin's ultimately seeking to take on the task alone—all this is highly important. But it is important only as a backdrop against which the crucial events of the story are played out. To recount these events in chronological order at the outset would be to put unnecessary information in the way of the reader before the significance of the events is understood, thus delaying the planting of the hook.

The motivations of the individual characters for visiting Heller also cannot conveniently be told at the outset.[4] For one thing, many of the events take place simultaneously or nearly so and thus cannot possibly be told in strict chronological order anyway. In addition, to a very large extent the ordering of the events in real time is simply not relevant to the story; whether Character A visited Heller two weeks ago and Character B visited him only last week, for the most part makes no difference to the account. Further, note that each character's recounting of his or her motivation takes up at least a page or two of text; in fact, though there is some extraneous material included, the separate interviews of the suspects are virtually half the story (approximately 25 of the 50 pages). If all of this information were placed in strict chronological order, presented in the narrative prior to

---

[4] In Appendix A we present, in approximate chronological order (some facts are not clear), the background events affecting each participant up to the opening scene of the story, for consideration by the reader.

Goodwin's going to Heller's building and being unable to find him, this would be an enormous delay in the planting of the hook. In fact, without the hook already having been planted, the motivations of the characters as recounted in the narrative have no meaning to the reader because it is only against the fact of Heller's death that their motivations are examined for a possible motive for murdering him.

We conclude, therefore, that some instances of skewing between referential ordering and syntactic ordering of events is for rhetorical purposes, to establish and prolong tension and thus reader interest within the account.

4. *Missing Events in The Zero Clue*

In this regard it is highly important that two specific sorts of information are not related in the text at all. First, although Heller is found dead, the murder itself is not recounted as an event of the narrative, only admitted to in the joint interview. In fact, the reader is never told the precise means used (a gun is alluded to), or the details of the encounter between Heller and Ennis and any discussion they engaged in that led up to the murder. Second, earlier interactions between Wolfe and Inspector Cramer are not recounted, though they color the story significantly by influencing the manner in which their present relationship is conducted. Their relationship is a distrustful one, bordering on the adversarial. There are indications that Cramer is jealous of Wolfe, suspicious of him, suspecting that he is untrustworthy and underhanded. Wolfe for his part seems to consider Cramer (and the police in general) to border on the incompetent. When Cramer first appears on the scene at Wolfe's house, the reader has no reason to expect at that point that Cramer will be so negative and accusatory about Wolfe's possible involvement in the murder; there is a carryover from earlier dealings, not included in the text itself.

Consider first the fact that earlier history between Cramer and Wolfe is not recounted. While it would not be impossible to review such a history in each work, Stout (and he undoubtedly is not alone in this) depends upon an on-going relationship with the reader; most likely he expects (or at least hopes) that his readers will not be content with a single work, but will want to read others as well, and indeed it is the ongoing competition and antagonism between Wolfe and Cramer that is one of the attractions of the series. To repeat even in an extended summary manner such details would be to risk boring the reader by repetition (and possibly offending the reader by suggesting that he or she could not remember the earlier accounts). Further, recounting past events solely for the purpose of establishing details of relationship also threatens to slow down the story and thus reduce the tension involved.

The fact that the murder itself is not recounted is very interesting. In a way, the reader is invited to see events only as the viewpoint character (Goodwin) sees them. We see here a strong indication that Stout sees the world through people who have only human capabilities—readers are not omniscient and thus privy to all facts because Goodwin is not; the reader is not present as a witness to the murder because Goodwin was not; the reader is invited to participate in solving the puzzle because that is the task set for Goodwin (and more precisely, Wolfe, the real hero of the series).

Nevertheless, the omission of this crucial event is striking. If all events of the rhetorical structure of the text are considered, this is the most dramatic, the most significant in terms of human value. Indeed, without the murder itself, there is no crime to be solved and thus no story. But it is apparent that the real story from Stout's point of view is not the crime itself, but the solving of the crime, so from the point of view of his purposes, the actual portrayal of the crime, while important as an inciting incident, is superfluous as an event and can be omitted from direct accounting.

We see once again, therefore, that the author's purpose in telling the story is crucial in influencing the form the narrative account takes.

5.   *The Influence of Author's Purpose on Text Presentation*

Consider further the influence of the author's worldview on the form of a text. Although Stout's work is of the 'detective' genre, there are indications that in a real sense, contrary to what we said above, it is in fact not the solving of the crime that is the point of the story. It is the adventure of solving the crime that the reader is invited along on, to be sure, and without the tension involved in solving the crime there is little interest and in fact no story. But Stout's purpose apparently lies even beyond that. After Ennis has confessed and been arrested, the last sentences of the story *The Zero Clue* are as follows (p. 103):

> ... Susan Maturo was up against me, gripping my lapels.
> "Tell me!" she demanded. "Tell me! Was it him?"
> I told her promptly and positively, to keep her from ripping my lapels off. "Yes," I said, in one word.
>   Two months later a jury of eight men and four women agreed with me.

The final sentence here is actually not part of the storyline, at least not if the storyline is seen as solving the puzzle of the perpetrator of the crime. But its inclusion is not insignificant, and in fact it might be argued that it is its absence that would provide material requiring analysis. Note that such a pattern is not characteristic of only this story. In the story *Invitation to Murder*, the perpetrator of the crime (again a murder) confesses under

Wolfe's effective questioning and is arrested. The last sentence of the story (omitting irrelevant details here) is the following (p. 53):

> Months have passed, and only last week a jury convicted Theodore Huck of first-degree murder. ...

It appears, then, that in at least these two stories Stout's concern is not only with solving the crime, but with seeing justice served. What is particularly interesting in these examples is that Stout-as-author does not intervene to add these comments as a moral; rather, the form of the text itself is such that the comments are put into the mouth of the viewpoint character, Goodwin (note the use of *me* in the first example). These are not, therefore, strictly speaking narrative comments, though they do have the function of adding a moral value to the account.

Finally, we may consider Stout's purpose as being reflected in the nature of his characters. The characters he chooses to employ are multi-faceted, complex, with what might be considered both good and bad characteristics. And just as we see in the expression of the purposes of Stout himself, his characters also have purposes which the events in which they participate are intended to achieve. There is much to be said on this topic, but we consider only a few examples here.

In Appendix C we include a summary of some of the major characteristics of the recurring characters as portrayed in these works, regarding which only a few comments are made here. Note first that it is characteristics such as these (in addition to naming, of course) which allow the individuals to remain identifiable across the series. We expect each instantiation to manifest the qualities we have come to see in the individuals from other contact with them; they all have a history, part of which they share and build upon (e.g., recall the discussion of prior contact between Wolfe and Cramer above).

Consider first the hero of all the stories of the series, Nero Wolfe. Although he is very much concerned with bringing criminals to justice, he manifests a robust appetite, with expensive and exotic tastes, and he is also fat and lazy. Such is his approach to life that he tends to shun work, though as a human being a major purpose behind his vocation is gaining the resources to live a satisfactory life-style (thereby forcing Goodwin as his assistant to often take the initiative to insure that the business continues to have an income). Once his reluctance is overcome and he is underway, Wolfe has a characteristic manner of going about investigation, often including a series of private interviews with the suspects, followed by a joint meeting with all of them at once. At the latter meeting typically he includes some sort of threat that the perpetrator of the crime will be revealed by other means if he or she does not confess, and a confession always follows. In short, the notion of human purpose is clearly seen in Wolfe's actions themselves, in addition to the fact that his personal characteristics and behavior are themselves characteristic of normal human beings, thus reflecting Stout's view of life.

Or consider Jack Ennis' character in the particular story under examination here. He is the murderer, the villain, but not a person lacking redeeming qualities. Stout portrays him as very intelligent, an inventor, a creative individual. He is ambitious, seeking fame and fortune to justly compensate him for his brilliance. Clearly on the negative side, however, he is a liar, concealing the truth in his interviews with Wolfe in an attempt to protect himself against discovery. And he is a vengeful man, whose anger at rejection and desire to retaliate ultimately are the driving force behind his murder of Heller. Of course, a detective story without a villain would be a rather colorless account, and in fact the perpetrator of the crime would have to act out of character if the crime were committed for reasons that are not evident from the nature of the individuals and the situations involved. Nevertheless, in his portrayal of Ennis (and others in the stories as well, who, though not the ones committing the crimes, show such traits as rage, jealousy, deceit, etc.) Stout shows that the world he wishes to convey is one which is populated by individuals who are not perfect; it is, in fact, like the real world.

Finally, consider the viewpoint character, Archie Goodwin. The important role Goodwin plays colors every story and most events within them; without Goodwin, Wolfe would not be a success for all his brilliance. Goodwin's mixed feelings regarding the police are reflected in his comments and self-revealed attitudes, as well as his actions in seeking to assist Wolfe in solving the crime while at the same time being less than fully cooperative with the police. His attitude toward women shows itself in his actions as reflected in his self-reported evaluations of beauty, his desires to complete his work so he can pursue his social life, his politeness. But Goodwin also is less than perfect, even though the story is told from his point of view. He at times resorts to deceit himself to get Wolfe to act; he is envious that Wolfe gets the credit for work he, Goodwin, played a major role in; he resents Wolfe's demands on his time and energies. Like the other characters portrayed, Goodwin is a normal human being.

6. Conclusion

In this paper we have examined the relationship between the linguistic form of a text, and the referential form being encoded by the text. We have found that skewing exists, so that the linguistic portrayal does not match the referential facts; some events are narrated in an order other than that in which they occurred, and some events (even highly significant ones) are not included in the narrative at all. We conclude that it is the author's purposes which influence the form of a given text, including such matters as which events to portray, and in what order. The author's purposes have influence also in the sorts of characters who serve as the cast, and in their own purposes and in the ways they interact with one another. Finally, there is some indication that the purpose of the author manifests itself in statements reflecting the worldview of the author.

We conclude, therefore, that text analysis involves more than simply investigating the linguistic (grammatical) structure of a given text. Information not found in the text itself, but still part of its referential structure, must be considered for a full analysis.

REFERENCES

Pike, Kenneth L., and Evelyn G. Pike. 1983. *Text and Tagmeme*. Norwood, NJ: Ablex
Stout, Rex. 1964 [1934]. *Fer-de-Lance*. New York, NY: Pyramid.
—————. 1954 [1952]. *Three Men Out*. New York, NY: Bantam Doubleday Dell.
—————. 1975 [1947]. *Too Many Women*. New York, NY: Viking.

APPENDIX A

Chronology of *The Zero Clue* by Characters

The following is a listing of events pertaining to each character which took place prior to the beginning of the text and revealed only later. The reference point is the opening scene, which chronologically takes place at the point indicated by TEXT STARTS. Here among the main characters Heller is abbreviated as H, Goodwin as G, Wolfe as W, Inspector Cramer as C; the six suspects are abbreviated as follows: Winslow (Wi), Maturo (M), Tillotson (T), Ennis (E), Abbey (A), Busch (B). Where information is available regarding precise time in relation to the opening of the narrative, that information is indicated.

Leo Heller

math prof at Underhill College
applied probability theory to events   at least 5 years ago
checked results after two years = 86.3% correct
wrote up results for magazine
requests came in in response to article
enabled a woman to find lost $31,000
resigned from UC to go full-time, accepting clients only
    in person   3 years ago
corporation president hired W to find information leak

                 'some months ago'

W's research slow
president approached H
H identified person, who later confessed
president admitted W supplied most information H used,
    should be paid
W steamed, told G not to send bill
G overruled W (looking after W)
W still angry at H
H phoned W's office, reached G, expressed idea that client
    may have committed a crime   1 day ago
H received return call from G to set up appointment to meet
    10:15 next AM
next AM H ate sausage and griddle cakes for breakfast
H went to office at 9:55

TEXT STARTS

Archie Goodwin (W's assistant)
    took call from H, put him off to consult with W   1 day ago
    found W with orchids, angry about thrips
    reported on H's call
    W refused job angrily
    G phoned H to report negatively
    G negotiated meeting to get basic facts from H
    appointment set for 10:15 next AM

TEXT STARTS

John R. Winslow [some uncertainty here about precise chronological
    details]
    aunt inherited from husband killed six years ago in a hunting
        accident at which Wi present   6 years ago
    Wi in debt, seeking to borrow from bank
    at aunt's death, Wi will receive inheritance
    Wi went to H to get prediction as to possible time of aunt's
        death—loan cost determined by time of pay-back
    Wi supplied H with information regarding wife's family
        history and life-style

TEXT STARTS

Susan Maturo
    worked at hospital (registered nurse)
    explosion at hospital killed 302 (including M's fiancee),
        others injured, M escaped   'about a month ago'
    2 weeks later M sought work elsewhere, found none
                        about 2 weeks ago
    studied papers, looking for clues as to bomber
    read about H
    worked all night preceding night
    went to H for lead (this her first visit)
    while waiting, felt idea crazy, left

TEXT STARTS

Mrs. Albert Tillotson
    received suspicious letters, blackmail—six in all,
        anonymous, quotations
    went to H to find out who sent them (went twice)

TEXT STARTS

Jack Ennis [some uncertainty here about precise chronological details]
 inventor/diemaker, presently unemployed
 held patents for 6 inventions, none marketed
 1 invention lacked crucial modification, went to H for help
  (3 times)
 went to hospital with x-ray machine modification, committee
  rejected it
 planted bomb in hospital
 H discovered E was bomber [chronology not clear]
 on his way to see H, E passed G and M talking in lobby [told
  in real time]
 E realized that H knew
 E met with H, confronted him
 H arranged pencils
 E killed H, stuffed body in closet, gun beneath

TEXT STARTS

Agatha Abbey
 executive editor of *Mode* magazine
 A's fashion predictions in past year erroneous
 contacted H for help in predicting fashions   10 days ago
 H came to her office to look at information
 A phoned H the next day, H agreed to proceed, would reply
 in about 1 week   9 days ago
 A phoned H 'yesterday', H told her to come   1 day ago

TEXT STARTS

Karl Busch
 unemployed
 went to H to get information on horse races
 after 3 visits, H agreed on 3-horse test
 3 winners, including *Zero* as longshot

TEXT STARTS

Inspector Cramer
 became aware of H's death
 investigated

found H dead, shot through heart, body stuffed
in closet, gun beneath
found G had been at H's office earlier
'on his way down' went by W's house

TEXT STARTS

APPENDIX B

Chronology of Events in *The Zero Clue* as Related in the Text

Abbreviations here are the same as those used in Appendix A.

G has checks to deposit in vicinity of H's office [p. 53]
G goes to H's office building
doorman in lobby about to challenge G
Wi passes G on his way to elevator
M steps out of elevator
G introduces himself to doorman
doorman queries G, requests Wi's autograph
    M stops and turns
    Wi sticks his head out of elevator doorway
Wi goes on up
G explains his presence to doorman [p. 54]
FLASHBACK explaining G's presence in H's building [see text]
G and M talk briefly [p. 57ff]
A enters lobby, allowed by doorman to proceed upstairs
G and M discuss possibility of her hiring Wi
E enters lobby, goes to elevator without doorman intervening
rushed for time, G and M cannot finish discussion, M leaves
G goes up to H's suite, arrives at 10:28 [p. 60]
G goes to H's private office, rings bell twice, no answer
door ajar, G pushes it open, enters, calls H's name
G looks around room [many details] while waiting
G sees scattered pencils laying on desk
G goes to waiting room, leaving H's office door ajar as he found it
G finds Wi, A, E, B, T waiting to see H
G asks if H has been there, receives negative reply
G returns to H's office, finds no change
G leaves building, takes taxi home, arrives in time for scheduled meeting
    with Wi [11 AM?]

C arrives at Wi's home [6 PM] [p. 62]
G lets C in, they join Wi who is watching TV
G asks Wi what he is doing for H
Wi replies 'nothing'
C asks why G was in H's office that AM
G interrupts to say 'exploring'
Wi and C both exasperated at G
Wi asks C if H is dead
C confirms
Wi asks G if G killed H
G denies, summarizes his visit to H's office
C reports details uncovered by investigation
C reports envelope found in H's desk for Wi, $500 inside
Wi denies involvement, takes envelope
C summarizes findings as pointing finger at Wi [pp. 64ff]
C reports other suspects left waiting room at intervals [p. 65]
G corrects C's model of display of pencils [p. 67]
C says pencils say 'NW'
Wi goes to bookshelf, reads briefly while others wait
Wi returns to desk, places book in drawer, locks it
C says Wi himself didn't kill H, nor did G, but Wi involved, hence
    pencils
police officer at murder scene contacted by phone, confirms that eraser
    forcibly removed from one pencil
Wi claims to know meaning of pencil message, refuses to divulge it,
    requests all six suspects be assembled
C calls to arrange assembly [p. 71]
police interview Wi, M, E, A, B [p. 71]
while eating dinner, Wi reads documents of interviews, in C's company
'return to [Wi's] office' [from restaurant?]
Wi, C, G assembled, with Stebbins as stenographer

Wi interviewed privately
complains that interrogation unconstitutional
W summarizes from document
Wi confirms with some give and take
W asks Wi to repeat all conversations with H
Wi does so, with some phone interruptions
Wi leaves

C complains that W has no real leads, that pencils indicate 'NW'
W gives hint that number 6 is involved, asks that interviewers be alert

for it

C points out Wi's uncle died 6 years ago and left him 6 cents, but both
    being investigated already

[precise chronology of following in relation to events not clear]

T visits H's office [p. 80]

offers bribe to guarding officer for files to be unlocked and her left alone
    in office

officer arrests T

M brought in by Stebbins for private interview [p. 75]

M accepts beer, licks lips, pleasing W

M repeats account of visit to H

W accuses M of thinking H planted hospital bomb and killing H [p. 78],
    or maybe planting bomb herself

M's denial is demonstrative

W requests names of 6 close friends of M killed in blast

messenger enters with information that T has been found [she had been
    missing]

M excused

officer who had been left guarding H's office enters, reports T's visit and
    attempted bribe

T interviewed privately [p. 81]

T lies regarding motive for seeing H, claiming she was seeking help in
    choice for son's college

T states that she was worried about details divulged to H regarding her
    son, went to H's office to retrieve them

T denies accusation of attempted bribery

T accused of lying, bribery; threatened with arrest

T admits search really for blackmail letters [p. 84]

W requests recess for dinner [now past midnight]

E interviewed privately [p. 85]

A interviewed privately [p. 88]

W cites earlier statements

    A had never seen H before

    A refused to state motive for seeing H

    A lied about motive, finally saying she was seeking information
        regarding stolen ring

A tells the truth

names of 6 competitors for A's job requested

A walks out, angry
C accuses W of having no genuine leads, simply prolonging investigation

B interviewed privately [p. 92]
Stebbins' seating pattern indicates he thinks B is culprit
W requests details of B's discussions with H
B replies that such detailed report not possible, told to do the best he can
B relates betting scheme, longshot winner Zero
W indicates by posture and closed eyes that something has struck his
    attention [p. 95]
B puzzled by W's actions—asleep? having a fit?
W asks B to be removed temporarily
W self-critical, asks that all 6 be brought in

all 6 interviewed together [p. 96]
27 people in all in attendance
W relates contact with H
    that H had called to report suspicion that client had committed serious
        crime
    asked by H to investigate, W declines, G pursues on his own
    W reports G's findings
all 6 asked to look at arranged pencils
W says pencils contain clue, reports consulting math book—India
    numbering system corresponds to 3x2 = 6
W self-critical for missing point of eraser—Hindus use dot for zero, not
    'times', so pencils represent 302 not 3x2 = 6
M reacts, W responds affirmatively—302 died in explosion
police in room react, they have been unable to solve explosion crime
W points out H's pencils indicate the crime, not the criminal
W asks each of 6 to respond if they have been at the hospital before
    T: no
    E: no
    M skipped [known she had worked there]
    B: no
    A: visited a patient there 2 years previously only
    Wi: no
W points out only M without denial
W requests that C arrest all 6

hold them without bail
assemble all available who are/were associated with the hospital
interview as to whether any of 5 who denied had been there
E interrupts—admits he went to hospital with machine, rejected
W asks E if he had ever invented a bomb
E evasive
W accuses E
C interrupts to arrest E
E dives at W, restrained by group
M grabs G, asks if E is bomber
G replies yes
2 months later jury agrees

APPENDIX C

Recurrent Character Traits in *Nero Wolfe* Series

In this summary chart we present a summary of details of consistent characterization of major participants in the works examined. Page numbers refer to the paperback editions listed in footnote 2; the presence of three dots (...) indicates that further reference was found in the same work which are not included here.

	Fer-de-Lance	The Zero Clue	Invitation to Murder	This Won't Kill You	Too Many Women
Nero Wolfe					
diet					
enjoys exotic foods	54	54,85		105,119	57,79,93 ...
separates work/eating		71	31,34		
enjoys beer	5,6,18 ...	62,74	7	119	20,122,125 ...
size					
massive	5,8,18 ...	85	1	105	72
special chair needed			1,8,36	105,108,143	93
home elevator	16,118	61			100,133
orchid hobby	15,35,22 ...	54	1,21		36,67,100 ...
personality					
brusque		62,76	1,31,34,35		

	Fer-de-Lance	The Zero Clue	Invitation to Murder	This Won't Kill You	Too Many Women
adversarial with police	23ff,36ff	64-70,74,98			100
manner at insight	11	95			125,136,151
subdued gestures	169	96			
lazy	191		1,2,19...		
characterization of Goodwin					
insubordinate		97		141	
good observer		97		112	
Archie Goodwin					
role as employee					
important in W's career		54	4	117	1
hiring W = hiring G		56		117	
does preparatory work	11,31ff	59	1ff	117ff	
character					
enjoys women	60,137ff	58,59,60 ...	11,13,20	104,107,132	10
highly observant		67,81	8,28		
Inspector Cramer					
gruff		62,101	46		
antagonistic to W		62ff	45ff		105,134,166

DATE DUE